SUPER HANDYMAN'S
Fix and Finish
Furniture
Guide

Books by Al Carrell

GOLF IS A FUNNY GAME
SUPER HANDYMAN'S ENCYCLOPEDIA OF HOME REPAIR HINTS
THE SUPER HANDYMAN'S BIG BIKE BOOK
SUPER HANDYMAN'S FIX AND FINISH FURNITURE GUIDE

SUPER HANDYMAN'S
Fix and Finish Furniture Guide

AL CARRELL

PRENTICE-HALL, INC.
Englewood Cliffs, New Jersey

This book is
lovingly dedicated
to *Jean*
who nagged me into becoming
the Super Handyman

Super Handyman's Fix and Finish Furniture Guide
by Al Carrell
Copyright © 1975 by King Features Syndicate, Inc.
All rights reserved. No part of this book may be
reproduced in any form or by any means, except
for the inclusion of brief quotations in a review,
without permission in writing from the publisher.
Printed in the United States of America
Prentice-Hall International, Inc., London
Prentice-Hall of Australia, Pty. Ltd., Sydney
Prentice-Hall of Canada, Ltd., Toronto
Prentice-Hall of India Private Ltd., New Delhi
Prentice-Hall of Japan, Inc., Tokyo

10 9 8 7 6 5 4 3 2 1
Library of Congress Cataloging in Publication Data
Carrell, Al
    Super handyman's fix and finish furniture guide.
    Includes index.
    1. Furniture-Repairing.   2. Furniture finishing.
I. Title.
TT199.C37   684.1'044   74–22216
ISBN 0–13–875997–9

Introduction

A Word About This Book

This book is written for the person who has never tried to fix or finish a perfectly good piece of furniture . . . "good," that is, except for a broken leg, loose rung, peeling veneer, bullet hole or other minor flaw!

Nearly every home I've ever visited has at least a few odd pieces of furniture that are beat up and need help or else have fallen out of favor and need rethinking. Even at the White House, almost every First Lady has sent at least a chair or two over to some little old furniture man to be refinished—maybe to match the President's new Cabinet. When you get through paying for White House changes via the IRS, you may not have enough loot left to refinish the things around your own house. Professional furniture fixers and finishers are expensive . . . even the little old man around the corner from the White House.

So for lack of funds, that chair in the dining room continues to snag your wife's hose (maybe her nylons, too). The family Bible must stay in a particular spot on the coffee table to hide the white ring. And Aunt Gussie Lou's highboy is placed high in the attic because the veneer is peeling.

It doesn't have to be. Probably all of the changes you

might contemplate are things that you could do—with a little information, the proper tools, and a lot of guts.

Time was, when all the furniture makers and remakers had closely guarded secret methods to achieve all the fix-and-finish results you're going to learn about. Their approach to each task was considered the "only" way . . . and their ways were often good. However, modern chemicals and tools have taken all the mystery and much of the work out of this endeavor. And it's no longer a task to be done only by the elite. My aim is to show you the way-to-go on fixing and finishing from the removal of nicks and stains to the finest luxury finishes. I'll also throw in some ideas for furniture projects you can build yourself, from scratch.

As a nonprofessional in furniture fixing and finishing, you're probably wondering what you can tackle safely. Well, a word about antiques: "Don't!"

You've probably already gathered that I'm not a lover of antiques . . . (except for my wife, Jean, who is not really getting older, just better). But we have picked up some antique furniture along the way, and so, along the way, I have picked up a little knowledge about antiques.

First of all, I learned that "antique" as applied to furniture doesn't just mean "old." It must be handmade, be representative of the maker, and be over a century old. The age of one hundred years really has nothing to do with it. It's just that the antique designers and craftsmen started mechanizing back about 1830 or so.

This is why, until you have had a chance to try your hand on a less valuable piece of furniture, you shouldn't tackle the restoration of a priceless antique. You just might render it worthless. As a rule of thumb, avoid any piece where the *original* veneer, grain, finish, hardware, or what-have-you is of the least historical interest. The antique dealers who pay big money want to be sure that as much of a piece as possible is original. And that old cabinet may be worth more with its warped back panel than if you replaced it with snazzy new veneer that made it look like a million dollars. Collectors turn up their noses if the original design has been altered, or if as much as 10 percent of the piece has been replaced with new parts. (By the way, where did you get a priceless antique? Most of my friends' heirlooms can be dated as Early Roosevelt.)

But don't convince yourself, either, that a "period" piece will remain beyond your eventual capabilities. After you gain a little confidence, skill, and knowledge, you may be able to increase both the value and beauty of a hundred-year-old Duncan Phyfe console. But in the meantime, the noncollector like me—and probably like you—should look for potential beauty, the possibilities for restoration, and the utility of the piece. The last considerations are age and history.

Most of the other books on furniture refinishing (yes, there are others) suggest that you not waste your time, effort, and good clothes on a piece of pine furniture or one that has no character. To that, I say, Poppycock! (Actually, that isn't what I would say, but I have my reputation to consider!) Probably the best first project is a new unfinished piece that requires only some imagination and a wax or varnish finish. Even if it's a $9.95 unfinished pine chair, you may get $100 worth of pleasure from putting a glazed finish over a shocking pink base coat. Whatever you do will be well worth the effort. You'll have made a blah piece of furniture look great, and this will be a source of pride to you, a reason for compliments from your friends and relatives, and probably a saving to your pocketbook. If it makes you feel proud every time you pass it in the hall, it's got to have been a good investment of time and effort.

However, this book will take you from that first necessary step on to more advanced work. As we move ahead, though, we don't get technical. We stick to the basics—the kind of plain talk everyone can understand. Once you get the taste of victory—it *will* look great—then go on to the chore of refinishing something a little more elderly from the attic. After that, it's a matter of practice, testing various techniques, expanding your inventory of tools, and gaining confidence.

If you don't have any old junk around to restore, don't despair. Every seven seconds a "Garage Sale" sign is posted on some neighbors' front lawn. Add to that the unclaimed freight auctions, church bazaars, Salvation Army and Goodwill Industries stores, and Aunt Gussie Lou's attic, and you have a ready source of cheap (sometimes even inexpensive) furniture for you to enhance.

An old piece with no pedigree offers you an opportunity to go creative. For example, we have this William and Mary hall tree that came from an English sporting house. It's where Shakespeare once hung his hat on a Saturday night. And the Windsor chair—would you believe . . . ?

Another fringe benefit to furniture doctoring is that it's fantastic therapy. It's hard to dwell on problems of the office while you're knee-deep in sawdust. One psychiatrist prescribes it at group-therapy sessions for all his patients—and has a dandy repair business on the side, fixing his colleagues' couches.

Now, it's not all going to be easy work. Making a pine box look good with a coat of paint is duck soup. However, removing somebody else's duck soup from a table top may become quite a chore. Nevertheless, if you'll go ahead and tackle a few projects, you can seek your own level of difficulty.

The biggest reason why furniture projects don't work out is wrong diagnosis. Either you didn't properly identify the wood, the spot, the old finish, or the problem. Even doctors sometimes come up with the wrong diagnosis, so don't feel bad. You may have to bury your mistake in the attic, but chances are you'll just have to start over. But mental attitude is an important quality in the furniture fix-and-finish game. Go into the task with the idea that it's going to be fun. It won't *all* be, but mainly it is. Furniture wizardry is a combination of a little manual labor, chemical action, and often your own creative flair. Whether you're going into this as a hobby, a treatment, or just to try to avoid another whiplash suit from the collapsible Chippendale in the drawing room—enjoy it!

Many of the tricks and shortcuts included have never been published before. But before you start to throw accolades in my direction, you should know that most of these hints and tricks are not mine. Some are from readers of my syndicated newspaper column. Others are from craftsmen and gurus in the furniture field who have been kind enough to share their expertise (and sometimes a cup of coffee) with me.

And speaking of experts, I know you're out there. Some are disguised as grandmas, Uncle Harrys, amateur furniture builders, and no telling what else. As you experts go through this book, you'll find your way may differ from my way. Great! If you have a way of doing a particular chore that differs from mine and works well for you, stick to it . . . in fact, drop me a note and let me try it, too!

For you nonexperts who will get "expert" advice, once you get started, don't worry. Even if they tell you you're doing it all wrong, the methods talked about here have all worked well for somebody else—and certainly will for you.

Approach each project with the idea it'll be fun . . . and it will be. Once you've done your first fix-or-finish project, you're entitled to consider yourself an expert—and you'll be able to advise others, just as I'm doing. When you get through the book, you'll be ready to tackle just about anything on four legs or three, in wood, plastic, metal, or bamboo.

If you get into the category of antique restoration, it can even be profitable. (You can even get into making your own antiques, and be set up for life—in Sing Sing.) And you're bound to come up with some new tricks of your own. If you'll share them with me, I'll in turn share 'em with a few million fellow furniture fiddlers through the column. Keep those cards and letters coming in!

—Al Carrell

Contents

Part One

REPAIRS

There's nothing worse than to end up with a beautiful shiny piece of furniture that's taken a week out of your life, only to see it collapse when it's put to use. So the first step toward reviving a piece of furniture is to see that it's sound structurally. If it's not, then you'll need to make repairs—most of which are operations you'll be able to do. If, however, there is a turned rung, and you don't have a lathe, you may have to take the problem to that little old cabinetmaker.

So it would seem that a super-close inspection is called for. Here's a check list:

1. Is it level? Be sure it's on a flat surface for the check.
2. Are there loose joints? Remove all drawers and check the frame to see if there's any wiggle. Check doors for play. While the drawers are out, see if they are loose at the joints.
3. Examine all surfaces for cracks, dents, or any other wounds.
4. If it has veneer, go over it to see if there are loose or nicked edges, blisters, or dents.
5. Any fractures? Be particularly careful in checking rungs and legs for splits or breaks.
6. Is all the hardware still there?
7. Make sure the drawers and doors work properly.
8. Examine all flat surfaces for any warp.
9. Examine it to see if the old finish is shot. If you like the finish it has, no matter how grungy it looks, skip to Part Two and see if you can apply first aid—not all surface scratches require a complete refinishing job. If the current finish can't be revitalized, a complete refinishing job means stripping off the old finish beforehand—all of which should keep you in Part Two for some time.

If you ran into several repairs, make a list of what needs to be done and plan it on a step-by-step basis.

(If the style doesn't grab you, then you *know* you'll have to saw off the legs or amputate the arms or whatever to make it look right. If it's got broken or missing parts, surgery or patch-up probably means you're forced to refinish.)

Chapter **1**

Chair Rungs

Almost every dining room set has one chair that has a snag place. You never think about it except just before company arrives, when you don't have time to fix it. You *do* have time to cover up the snag with either a small strip of clear tape or with a drop of clear fingernail polish. (Only trouble with that good idea is that the only way I can locate the snag spot is to have my wife sit down and sacrifice a pair of nylons.)

The most common ailment, however, is the loose rung. Usually this is just a matter of regluing. All surfaces to be glued should be cleaned. Otherwise, you may just be gluing one surface to a layer of wax—and that will last about seventy-one hours and twenty-seven minutes. This means you must remove all the old glue, both on the rung and in the hole.

This also means spreading the legs far enough apart to get the end of the rung out without breaking any other joints loose. Sometimes this isn't easy. One of the readers of my column suggested a lever arrangement made of scrap lumber as shown in Fig. C-1. It works well. It allows slow, steady pressure that lessens the likelihood of total collapse.

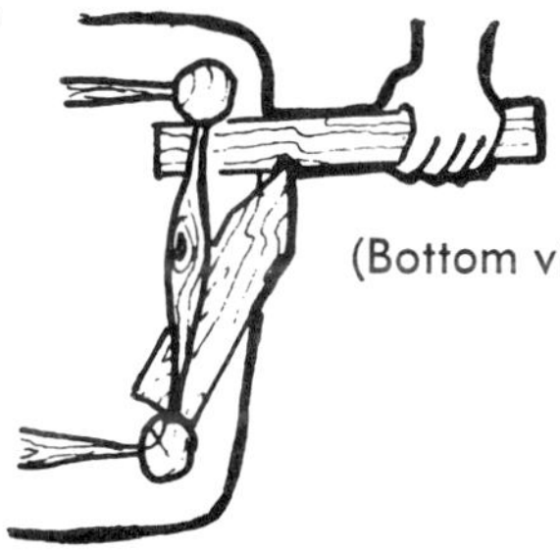

Fig. **C-1**   (Bottom view of chair)

To remove glue from inside the holes in dowel joints, make a sanding stick by wrapping a strip of sandpaper around another piece of dowel and gluing it in place. Then put the dowel in the chuck of your drill, and you can get all the dried glue out in short order.

Some older furniture glues can be dissolved with vinegar. If you're removing glue, you might give this a try before trotting out to find a stronger solvent. Heat the vinegar to a simmer, and then brush it on. If it's going to work, you'll know in about fifteen minutes. Then you can trot out to find a stronger solvent.

If the hole and rung are still a good fit, gluing and proper clamping will do the job. If not, here are a few tricks:

1. Plug the old hole by gluing a dowel in the hole. Cut it off flush. When the glue holding the dowel is set, drill a new hole just right for the rung.
2. Instead of squirting glue in a dowel hole and depending on the dowel to spread the stuff, you'll get a stronger joint if you brush the glue into the hole. A tiny artist's brush that you're not too fond of will give complete coverage.
3. Since dowels work better with a tight fit, one home handyperson suggests baking the dowels before using them in furniture. This gets all the moisture out. When the dowels are then placed in the holes and glued, they start to gain back some of the moisture and swell a tiny bit, giving a tighter fit. (But don't leave the dowels unattended in the oven. Some joker will come in and think the dowels are crumpets, though actually, they don't taste half bad.)
4. To make sure you get rung holes at the exact same height, make a template from a piece of notebook paper as shown in Fig. C-2. Wrap the template around each leg and mark the holes for drilling.

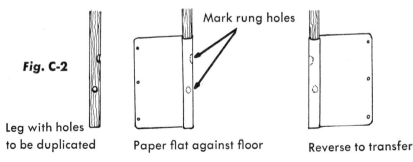

Fig. C-2

Leg with holes to be duplicated

Mark rung holes

Paper flat against floor

Reverse to transfer

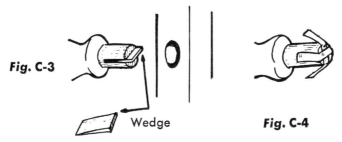

Fig. C-3

Wedge

Fig. C-4

5. Expand the end of the rung by cutting a slot in it and inserting a wedge, as shown in Fig. C-3.

6. Slightly roughened surfaces have better holding power than smooth ones, because the glue has more surface area to adhere to. So, use two narrow strips of cloth, as shown in Fig. C-4. Make sure the cloth won't stick out. Apply glue and insert the rung in place. The cloth increases tightness and gives more surface for the glue to grab hold of.

GLUES

Before we get down to further repairs, let's learn a little about glue. Most of the repairing is done with glue, or more properly, with adhesive. Rather than ramble on about adhesives, I've tried to put it all together in a super Adhesive Chart (see Table I).

Avoid cold rooms for gluing. Generally, adhesives work better in warmer temperatures. Also, if you just brought the piece of furniture in from a cold attic or garage, let the wood warm up to room temperature before starting the glue job.

Some handy glue spreaders are found all around the house. The saw-toothed blade from wax paper, foil, and other dispensers does a good job for this. A discarded pocket comb also spreads adhesives well.

Another trick is to fold over a piece of window screen to glide the glue. The secret is to have something that doesn't leave a smooth coat of goo behind it—the peaks and valleys make for better glue joints.

It's also a good idea to make sure the chair is on a level surface. Otherwise, it may be glued back stronger than an ox, but cattywampus. Weight in the chair also helps toward a more solid repair. We bought a set of encyclopedias for that purpose. *Aar* through *Maa* is about the right weight.

Table I
ADHESIVE CHART

Type	Uses	Preparation*
White glue (polyvinyl or PVA) like Elmer's	Interior cabinetwork where no moisture is expected.	Glue is ready to go. Be sure surfaces are dry and clean.
Hide glue (hot glue)	Same as above . . . the old-timer's favorite furniture glue.	Comes in both dry (flake) and liquid form—heat in glue pot or *old* double boiler.
Plastic resin	Indoor or outdoor furniture, where good clamping pressure can be applied and when joints are tight fitting. Good for veneers.	Mix powder with water according to directions.
Casein glues	Indoor or outdoor furniture. Especially good for oily woods like teak, rosewood, etc. Good for loose joints as it tends to fill gaps.	Mix powder with water according to directions.
Resorcinol	Great for outdoor or even underwater furniture.	Powder or liquid mixed with resin per directions.
Epoxy	Great for everything where cost is not a factor and where glue can be applied quicky.	Two components. Must be mixed equally, thoroughly, and according to directions.

* This is just the general idea on preparation. Always read and follow package directions.

How to Apply	Strength	Resistance to		Setting Time	Appearance When Dry
		Water	Heat		
Coat one surface and clamp for at least one hour.	fair	poor	poor	24 hours	clear
Apply while hot to both surfaces. When tacky, clamp and leave for 4 hours.	good	poor	poor	24 hours	almost colorless
Apply thin coat to both surfaces. Clamp tight for 18 hours.	good+	good+	good	24 hours	almost colorless
Apply thin coat to both surfaces and clamp for 8-10 hours.	good but brittle	fair	good	24 hours	clear to pale yellow
Apply thin coat to both surfaces. Clamp for 18 hours.	excellent	excellent	excellent	18 hours	dark reddish-brown
Apply according to directions, different for different kinds. Work fast.	super	super	very good	read the label	varies

No matter what method you've used, once the glue is applied and the rung is back in place, clamping pressure is needed.

Nearly all gluing requires the proper pressure to make sure the parts are held firmly together while the adhesive sets up. There are dozens of ways to apply such pressure. Many different types of clamps are available, and yet sometimes you'll need to set the brain in motion to come up with just the right way to exert gluing pressure. I've tried to cover the conventional clamps and will throw in a few brainstorms at the end.

C clamps — This is the most common type of clamp. They are inexpensive, versatile, and come in many sizes. C clamps can be used in conjunction with pressure blocks, rope, and other things to convert them to other clamping chores.

Pipe clamps — These are needed when a large tabletop has cracked and needs gluing back together. You buy the two pieces shown, and then fit in a length of ¾-inch pipe of any length. It's a good idea to keep several lengths of pipe on hand and use the one closest to the needed clamp width (Fig. C-5).

Fig. C-5

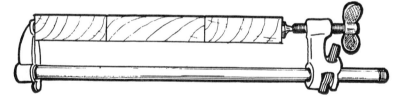

Bar clamps — They are used for the same type of clamping, but the flat bar is a permanent part of the clamp. They come in various sizes.

Hand-screw or wood clamps — These clamps have wooden jaws and a pair of screw handles. They can grip nonparallel surfaces since the jaws can adjust to many angles.

Spring clamps — They are sort of like large alligator clamps or clothespins. They have minimal pressure but are quick to clamp on.

Picture-framing or corner clamps — These are great for mitered joints. They can be fabricated in several ways other than the one shown (Fig. C-6).

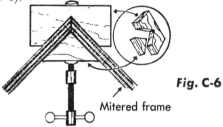

Fig. C-6

Mitered frame

Web, belt, or band clamps — Great for holding legs and rungs together, and are the easiest to apply. However, if you don't have one, you can rig up a tourniquet. A rope and a stick will do the job. A belt, or even last year's neckties will do. If you're stout, your belt may be big enough to make the trip around.

Figure C-7 shows the tourniquet-type clamp in place. If more than one joint is involved, put the tourniquet around all four legs.

Fig. C-7

Another reader uses a damp rope. As it dries, the rope begins to shrink a little, thus increasing the pressure which he claims compensates for the gradual stretching the rope goes through while in place.

Now for some of the tricky ideas, many of them thought up by the creative readers of my newspaper column (Figs. C-8, 9, 10, 11, and 12).

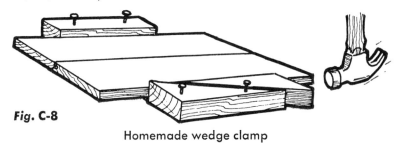

Fig. C-8

Homemade wedge clamp

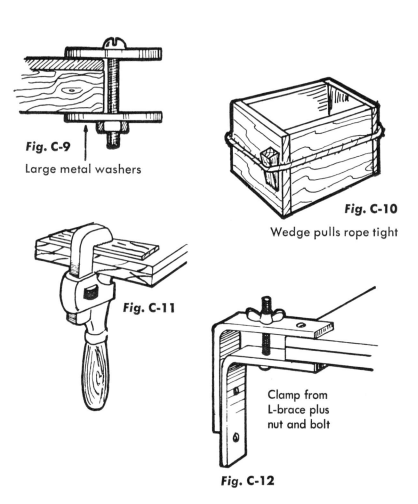

Fig. C-9

Large metal washers

Fig. C-10

Wedge pulls rope tight

Fig. C-11

Clamp from
L-brace plus
nut and bolt

Fig. C-12

Use the proper pressure, whether it be clamps or weights. When pressure is applied, some of the glue may be forced out. If it's going to ooze out on a finished surface, be prepared. Two thin strips of tape along a joint may be the answer (Fig. C-13). Also, be ready to wipe up glue that is forced out.

Give it time to set. Do follow the manufacturer's directions in mixing, applying, clamping, and waiting. He wants his glue to work and is trying to tell you how to make it work best.

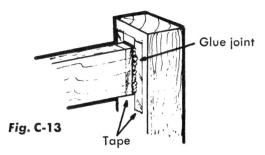

Glue joint

Fig. **C-13**

Tape

Chapter **2**

Cracked, Split, and Broken Parts

Chair seats also become split or cracked. Cracks and splits are usually with the grain and, therefore, run longways or diagonally. If it's a new crack or split, check to be sure it fits back together well. Then apply glue to both parts, put 'em back together, and clamp. If matching parts of the wood fiber are gone, and the fit is not that great, you'll have to use a casein glue that helps take up the gap. Clamping is a problem. Sometimes a C clamp or two will do the job. Be sure to pad the jaws so the clamp doesn't create a new repair problem. Tightly wrapped tape or string may have to do—or you may have to come up with your own creative clamping.

A partial split in a seat can often be repaired by getting glue down into the crack and clamping it back together. The success depends on: (1) Your making sure the split is such that the seat can be pressed back together with a perfect fit; (2) There's no dirt, wax, or whatever down in the crack; and (3) You can get the adhesive in to completely cover all surfaces inside the crack. This last step is best accomplished by flexing the seat back and forth, as shown in Fig. R-1. This opens the split and lets the glue flow down in.

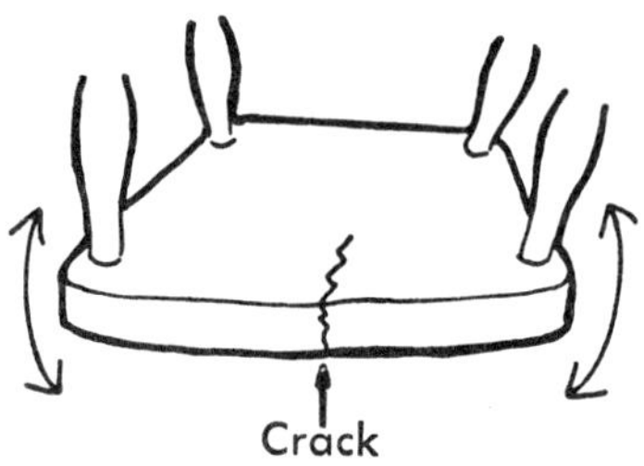

Fig. R-1

Crack

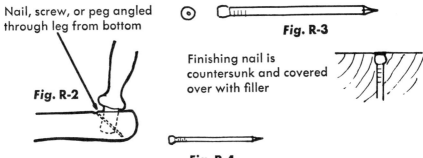

Nail, screw, or peg angled through leg from bottom

Fig. R-2

Fig. R-3

Finishing nail is countersunk and covered over with filler

Fig. R-4

This also sometimes splits the seat the rest of the way. But in some cases, it will pay you to go ahead and completely split the seat into two pieces. If there is dirt in the crack that you can't get out, or if fibers prevent a tight fit, you'll do a better job with a complete split. This also allows you to spread the glue properly.

Although not likely, it's possible for a chair seat to become warped. We'll take this up in the next chapter.

Loose legs, spindles, or braces are treated much the same way. In many cases, however, a leg that's loose has the advantage of joining the seat underneath where it's out of normal sight. This means the possible use of a nail, screw, or dowel angled into the seat and through the leg as shown in Fig. R-2.

The old master craftsman avoided the use of nails, screws, and mending plates. However, if you've taken my advice in the first place, you're not working on a priceless antique. If you need extra strength underneath, and a nail or screw will give it to you, be my guest.

Nails are not anywhere near as good in holding power as screws, because threads hold the wood against expansion and contraction. However, there are many times when the ease of installing and unobtrusiveness of nails makes them the best fastener.

The types most often used are the finishing nail (Fig. R-3) and the wire brad (Fig. R-4). Of course, upholstery nails are used on furniture, but that's a different bag (Chapter 17).

Nails are sized by penny, and the symbol is *d*—the same symbol used for "penny" in England. The following chart tells all about the finishing nail.

FINISHING NAILS

SIZE	LENGTH (INCHES)	GAUGE NO. (SHANK)	GAUGE NO. (HEAD)	APPROXIMATE NUMBER PER POUND
3d	1¼	15½	12½	880
4d	1½	15	12	630
6d	2	13	10	290
8d	2½	12½	9½	196
10d	3	11½	8½	124

(Finishing nails are available in 2d, 5d, 7d, 9d, 12d, 16d and 20d, but are considered nonstandard sizes and are not widely stocked.)

Wire brads come in lengths up to three inches.

I really recommend a pilot hole for nails in wood that is fairly hard. Getting a proper size drill bit need not be a problem. Snip the head off of a nail or brad the same size as the one you're using and chuck it in a twist drill. This will give you a pilot hole.

The most basic drilling tool is the power drill. However, it must be used properly or you'll end up in trouble.

There are advantages to an old style brace and bit (Fig. R-5). It's slow, sure, and a lot easier to control. A twist drill (Fig. R-6) has the same advantages for smaller holes. Even the ratchet drill will come in handy—plus the fact it has screwdriver blades, too.

I also recommend that glue also be used in joints in conjunction with the nails.

Screws come in wide varieties. Always provide a pilot hole for screws. The correct size pilot hole is very important.

The Wood Screw Chart (Table II) tells you about screws.

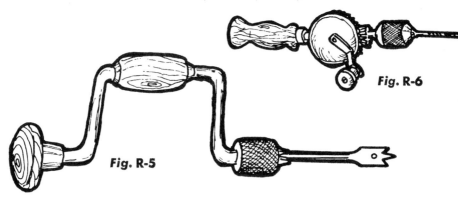

Fig. R-6

Fig. R-5

Table II
WOOD SCREW CHART

GAUGE NUMBER	DECIMAL DIAMETER	FRACTIONAL DIAMETER	SHANK HOLE		PILOT HOLE				THESE LENGTHS USUALLY AVAILABLE
			TWIST BIT	DRILL GAUGE	HARDWOODS		SOFTWOODS		
					TWIST BIT DIAMETER	DRILL GAUGE	TWIST BIT DIAMETER	DRILL GAUGE	
0	.060	1/16−	1/16	52	1/32	70	1/64	75	1/4"
1	.073	5/64−	5/64	47	1/32	66	1/32	71	1/4"
2	.086	5/64+	3/32	42	3/64	56	1/32	65	1/4"-1/2"
3	.099	3/32+	7/64	37	1/16	54	3/64	58	1/4"-5/8"
4	.112	7/64+	7/64	32	1/16	52	3/64	55	3/8"-3/4"
5	.125	1/8−	1/8	30	5/64	49	1/16	53	3/8"-3/4"
6	.138	9/64−	9/64	27	5/64	47	1/16	52	3/8"-1 1/2"
7	.151	5/32−	5/32	22	3/32	44	1/16	51	3/8"-1 1/2"
8	.164	5/32+	11/64	18	3/32	40	5/64	48	1/2"-2"
9	.177	11/64+	3/16	14	7/64	37	5/64	45	5/8"-2 1/4"
10	.190	3/16+	3/16	10	7/64	33	3/32	43	5/8"-2 1/4"
11	.203	13/64−	13/64	4	1/8	31	3/32	40	3/4"-2 1/4"
12	.216	7/32−	7/32	2	1/8	30	7/64	38	7/8"-2 1/2"
14	.242	15/64+	1/4	D	9/64	25	7/64	32	1"-2 3/4"
16	.268	17/64+	17/64	I	5/32	18	9/64	29	1 1/4"-3"
18	.294	19/64−	19/64	N	3/16	13	9/64	26	1 1/2"-4"
20	.320	21/64−	21/64	P	13/64	4	11/64	19	1 3/4"-4"
24	.372	3/8	3/8	V	7/32	1	3/16	15	3 1/2"-4"

Table II (continued)

DRILLING PILOT & SHANK HOLES

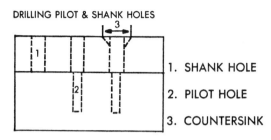

1. SHANK HOLE

2. PILOT HOLE

3. COUNTERSINK

Some random rules that help in the use of screws:

1. Use the proper size screwdriver. The tip should just fit in the slot and be just about as wide as the slot. The wrong size makes the screwdriver tip keep slipping, and is liable to chew up the screw slot.
2. If possible, select a screw that allows about two-thirds of its length to go into the base or second piece of wood.
3. In soft woods, drill a pilot hole only to about half the length of the screw.
4. Lubricate threads with candle wax or soap for easier installation. Neither will soak into the wood to leave a stain.
5. Like nails, use glue too with a screw. Just be sure the leg is tightly clamped in place before the pilot hole is drilled. It'll be a long, long time before that leg ever comes loose again. Weight in the seat is the key to pressure here. Use the encyclopedia up through *Zzy* this time.

Here are some mending plates and other hardware used underneath or out of sight to strengthen or hold furniture together. (Figs. R-7 through R-11).

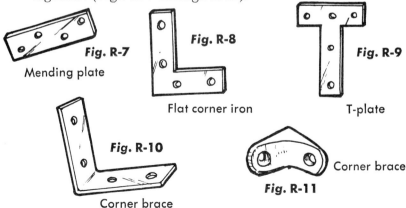

Fig. R-7
Mending plate

Fig. R-8
Flat corner iron

Fig. R-9
T-plate

Fig. R-10
Corner brace

Fig. R-11
Corner brace

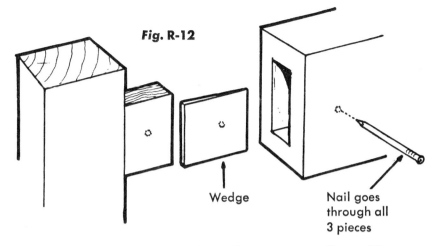

Fig. R-12

Wedge

Nail goes
through all
3 pieces

Sometimes, the parts of a chair—but more usually a table
—are not round as shown, but are of the tenon type, as in Fig.
R-12. The same general techniques can be used, with the
added advantage of being able to use shims to take up the slack
when need be. Cut the shims the same width as the tenon.

If there are *several* loose rungs, legs, and parts, it's really
better to dismantle all the parts and reglue the whole shebang.
By doing it all at once, you should end up with a stronger,
straighter chair.

The exceptions are the older pieces that have a sort of knob
on the end of rungs. Such a chair was made of dried wood fitted
into a hole in green wood. As the green wood dried, it shrank,
and the knob became impossible to remove. For those, you
should try a wood-expanding compound available at some
hardware stores. It causes the wood fibers to swell and hold
their new larger size. If this won't work, you may have to drill a
tiny hole as shown in Fig. R-13 and use a glue injector. With
this method, you need to jiggle the parts around to help spread
the adhesive as much as possible. Then clamp and pray.

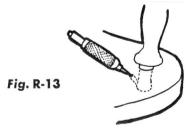

Fig. R-13

Cracked, Split, and Broken Parts   **17**

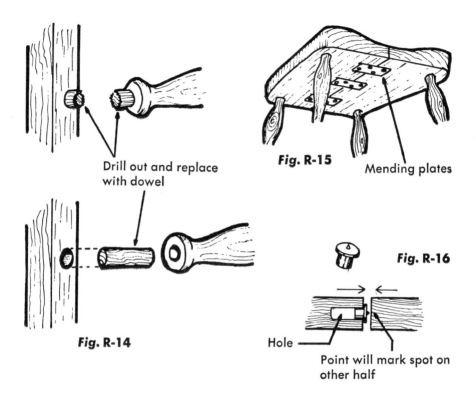

Drill out and replace with dowel

Fig. R-15   Mending plates

Fig. R-14

Fig. R-16

Hole

Point will mark spot on other half

Parts Broken in Sockets   The torture given a chair sometimes causes the rung to break off, leaving the tip or part of it in the hole. This isn't as bad as it may seem. Since that part goes inside anyway, dig or drill it out. Then if it's a round rung, fashion a short piece of dowel to fit into a hole drilled in the rung, as shown in Fig. R-14. A broken-off tenon is replaced the same way with a new false tenon glued in place.

A completely cracked seat allows for reinforced repairs. The reinforcements may be metal mending plates as shown in Fig. R-15. If it's a restoration of an old piece, however, you may not want hunks of metal showing even underneath. Doweling will give you a very strong repair with the reinforcements hidden within the wood. You must make sure that the dowels and their holes line up perfectly, however. Otherwise, you end up with a seat that won't line up.

This is a critical enough step that you should invest in a dowel-center set. Once the dowel holes are drilled in the first piece, the center is inserted as shown in Fig. R-16. The two pieces are then pressed together, and the point marks the exact spot on the mating part. (Be sure to check the tips on stronger dowel joints in the last chapter.)

After all holes are drilled and the dowels are inserted, give the seat a test hop before gluing. If they don't line up perfectly, don't be discouraged. See where the problem is. Then either shave a little off the side of the dowel or ream out the hole a little.

Once it's all lined up, glue it and clamp it and let it cure.

That leaves only one last chair malady—the mysterious case of the one short leg that causes a slight wobble. Finding the right leg to work on can drive you up the wall. Then after you find it, you may fiddle around for weeks and still have a wobbly chair. Sometimes you find the only way is to cut off the other three legs. This can lead to some funny-looking furniture, because you sometimes have to make several cuts. Chairs that are only nine inches off the ground aren't that popular.

Finding the short leg is a matter of detective work. I suggest using a level and also carefully measuring to find the errant leg—because a wobble can also result from one leg's migrating to a different angle than the other three (if so, that leg needs regluing). If you can get by with the addition of a tip, this may solve your problem. The tip may be one you buy as described in the later section on "footwork" (Chapter 15). It may be something you glue on the end to make it right. This could be nothing more than a piece of the cork liner found in some bottle caps or a little dot of felt. However, it might be a piece of wood made to match.

Sometimes a short chair leg can be remedied by taking a blob of wood putty and forming an extension. Usually all you need is a fraction of an inch. Putty can be formed to the shape of the leg, and when dry will stay in place. It can be touched up to look like the rest of the leg, and even if the match isn't 100 percent, there's not enough of it showing to be very glaring.

As for cutting, you not only have to cut the right amount off the other three legs, but if the legs are not straight up and down, the cut has to be at just the right angle so it's flat on the floor.

Put the chair on a level surface, and cut a scrap of wood to exactly fit under the short leg. Duplicate this scrap in thickness, and use the duplicate to carefully scribe a line all around the longer legs. Make your saw cuts just *below* the scribed lines. Pray as you saw. Use a rasp or sandpaper to shave off anything that needs to come off to make them even.

(If it didn't work out, hang onto the nine-inch-high chairs for the next school production of "Snow White and the Seven Dwarfs.")

Now let's look at table troubles.

Chapter 3

Tables, Bureaus, and Desks

Tabletops and chair seats can be one solid piece or can be two or more pieces jointed together. The legs may be joined together by pieces called aprons as in Fig. T-1. This type of base stands alone, and the top is then attached to this base. Other tables and many chairs have legs that are inserted into the top (Fig. T-2).

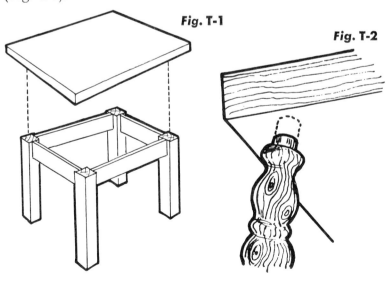

Fig. T-1

Fig. T-2

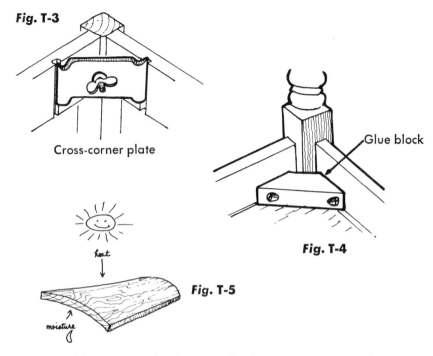

Fig. T-3

Cross-corner plate

Glue block

Fig. T-4

heat

Fig. T-5

moisture

Leg problems are solved in much the same way just described in the chair chapter. Wobblies can often be taken care of more easily because many tables have some sort of apron. This allows for the addition of glue blocks, metal brackets, or other devices between the *top* of the leg and the tabletop, all of which are hidden by the apron. Figs. T-3 and T-4 show these de-wobblers in place. You can figure out which best suits your purpose.

The big problem in tables nowadays is warping. This is generally caused by moisture differences within a piece of wood. Often it's because the top is partially sealed by the finish, while the bottom is bare. The top lets in a little moisture from the air while the bottom drinks in a lot. Generally warps are removed easier if the top can be removed first.

The idea is to equalize the moisture again. When this is done, the warped piece should come back to its original shape. A plain old warped board can be laid out on the ground in the sun with the concave side facing down. The heat of the sun will remove moisture from the top, and the soil and grass will add moisture to the bottom (Fig. T-5).

If the ground is dry, spread out wet towels underneath. The big kind you swiped from the Acme Plaza Hotel are fine. On a hot morning, you can remove a warp in a matter of hours.

If the idea of putting your tabletop out to pasture doesn't grab you, then you need another heat source. Heat lamps hanging a few inches above the convex side will do. Then brush a damp sponge over the hollow side. Or, if you have radiators for heat and it's wintertime, prop the top up so it's about four or five inches from a radiator. Again, have the curved-out side toward the heat source. Sponge the hollow side from time to time.

A small table could be placed above a radiator on wooden blocks. Several layers of wet hotel towels could then be placed in the hollow. Inside jobs may take a couple of days, but will get the job done. Some stubborn warps require removal of the finish on the hollow side so the moisture can get in.

If you're lucky and have patience, you can remove slight warps with clamps. Typical clamping set-ups are shown in Figs. T-6 and T-7, but you'll have to adapt clamping devices to suit your piece of furniture. The patience is needed because if you apply too much straightening pressure at once, the top may split. You should tighten just a little each day.

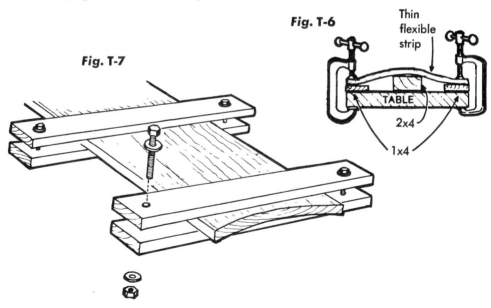

Fig. T-6

Thin flexible strip

TABLE

2x4

1x4

Fig. T-7

Fig. **T-8**

A combination of heat and moisture and clamping can work wonders. In fact, when there is twist as well as warp, it's a *must*.

Another de-warping method is to saw a series of straight lines on the bottom side of the table. A power saw is set so the blade leaves a kerf (cut) about halfway through the top. The cuts go with the grain and should come to within a couple of inches of the edges. Distribute the cuts so they are evenly spaced across the table bottom. When you've made enough cuts so the top can be clamped as shown in Fig. T-8 and made straight, you can then fill up the kerf with glue and thin slats of wood. Leave the clamps in place until the glue cures and until you've shaved off any part of the slats that might stick out. It's also a good idea to attach cleats across the bottom, either with glue or screws.

Now that the warp is gone, you want to do a couple of things immediately to prevent it from coming back. First, finish or seal *both* sides of the top. Next, reattach the top *securely*. Use plenty of glue blocks, screws, or whatever is called for to get it securely back in place. If the frame to which it's attached is lightweight, strengthen it where it won't show. This should be done before it's time to reattach.

Sometimes you need hardwood wedges in repairing furniture pieces underneath. There are some dandies available if

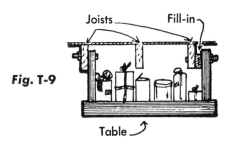

Joists_____ Fill-in

Fig. T-9

Table ⤴

you can sneak away a few springtype clothespins. Remove the springs, and cut off and shape as needed.

Wall paneling can be used very effectively to cover over a botched-up tabletop. Get the prefinished kind that doesn't have grooves but is smooth all over. It'll look groovy!

If you give up on a table that you just feel isn't worth redoing, convert it to a storage shelf. Attach it to the ceiling joists in the garage or attic as shown in Fig. T-9. (Is that what they mean by "turning the tables"?)

The next basic type of furniture piece is the bureau, chest, or desk.

BUREAU, CHEST, OR DESK

The special problem here is usually with drawers. They undergo a lot of pulling and pushing, which can result in loose joints. In most cases, you'll do a better job of repair if you take the drawer apart . . . or at least remove the loose part. This enables you to remove all the old glue so the new can penetrate the wood.

By knowing a little about how some furniture is put together, you'll be better equipped to repair it . . . maybe. Usually furniture is made by forming all the separate parts and joining them together. How *well* they are joined together makes the difference between a solid item and a death trap.

Desks and chests are basically boxes. They are usually either solid construction (Fig. T-10) or frame and panel construction (Fig. T-11).

Fig. T-10

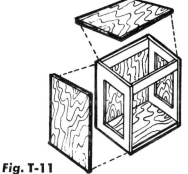

Fig. T-11

25

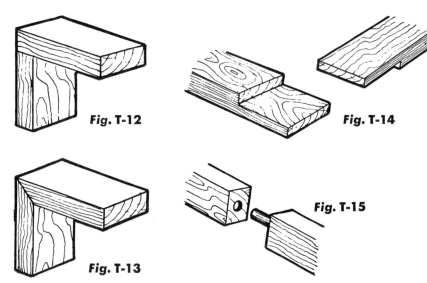

Fig. T-12

Fig. T-14

Fig. T-15

Fig. T-13

Drawers can be joined together by any number of different joints. Joints—the points where two parts are joined together—come in many varieties. The type of joint used depends on the strength needed and the appearance desired. The most common joints used in furniture are:

Butt joints (Fig. T-12)
Miter joints (Fig. T-13)
Lap joints (Fig. T-14)
Dowel joints (Fig. T-15)
Rabbet joints (Fig. T-16)
Mortise and Tenon joints (Fig. T-17)
Dovetail joints (Fig. T-18)

Fig. T-19 shows a combination of tongue and groove and dovetail joints used in one drawer.

Take care during the dismantling. Many drawers will be held together by dovetail joints *with* nails as shown in Fig. T-20. Examine to be sure no brads or nails have been driven into the joint. If they're there, they must come out first. Now place a scrap block of wood against the side and in the corner. Hammer against the block to force the joints apart.

Other drawers may have rabbet joints nailed together as shown in Fig. T-21, or tongue and groove joints with nails as shown in Figure T-22. Carefully remove the nails and the drawer will start to fall apart.

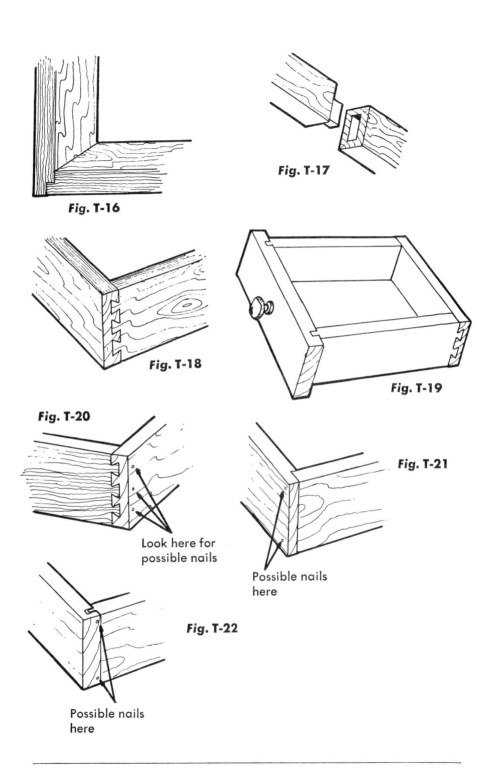

Fig. T-16

Fig. T-17

Fig. T-18

Fig. T-19

Fig. T-20

Look here for possible nails

Fig. T-21

Possible nails here

Fig. T-22

Possible nails here

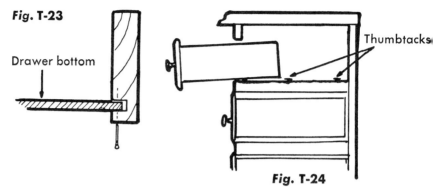

Fig. T-23

Drawer bottom

Thumbtacks

Fig. T-24

As mentioned earlier, remove all the old glue. Usually the pieces are easy to square up, but it's best if you use a square to be sure. One thing to remember about joints: the more area of the two parts that touch, the more glue can be used; thus, the stronger the joint.

If dovetails are involved, clamping isn't usually needed. However, lots of furniture folks use small brads to hold the joints in place while the glue sets up . . . and then leave 'em there to be sure (Fig. T-23).

Before the glue does set up completely, it's a good idea to test the drawer in place gingerly to be sure it fits. It's better to find out now than after the glue has done its thing.

The next drawer problem is that it doesn't go in and out properly. If it's too loose, it means either the drawer has become worn, or the rail is worn, or both.

Here you have to decide whether new rails are called for or whether to build up the wood that's worn away. The buildup is usually done by adding thin strips of wood. However, a few well-placed thumbtacks can sometimes solve the problem (Fig. T-24).

A sticking drawer is too big for its opening. However, it may be just temporarily swollen from moisture. The old light-bulb-in-the-drawer trick may dry it out enough to make it work smoothly. Or it may just need lubrication. Sprinkling talcum powder or rubbing a candle or a bar of soap provides good lubrication. Or if you have a candle mold, stir in a teaspoon of powdered graphite to the melted wax before pouring it in the mold. This will give you a super lube stick for wood.

Modern industry has come up with drawer hardware that is

easy to install and eliminates drawer problems. Tracks, suspension systems, rollers, and rail tapes all have their good points.

The nonstop drawer is also a problem. You pull it out, and Wham! It and the contents fall on your foot. The simple addition of a metal mending plate as shown in Fig. T-25 will put a stop to that jive. Whatever kind of drawer stop you rig up, remember that someday you may *want* to remove the drawer. So rig a stop that won't require an axe for removal.

Loose knobs can often be made tight again by taking up the gap with glue, a wedged-in toothpick, steel wool wrapped around the threads, or maybe even a plastic wall anchor, or "molly." If the hole is too badly reamed out, you may have to drill it out, glue in a dowel, and start over.

Whatever you resort to, it's a good idea to put an adhesive on the underside of the knob. This, plus the screw or bolt, will keep it from getting loose.

A sort of washer made of sandpaper can also be put behind a drawer knob that keeps getting loose. Put the grit side against the drawer. This will keep the knob from turning, and it will stay on tight. Of course, you must make the sandpaper circle small enough for the knob to hide.

One reader discovered that his wife was snagging her nylons even before she got them on. Seems the culprit was a screw holding the drawer knob on—its end stuck out inside the hosiery drawer and grabbed whatever was pulled forward. He solved the problem by gluing the plastic cap from a toothpaste tube over the screw.

A quick neat way to add dividers to drawers is to snip off sections of flat curtain rods to match the height of the divider. Mount these as shown in Fig. T-26. This gives you a slot for the divider. Sure beats cutting a slot in the side of the drawer.

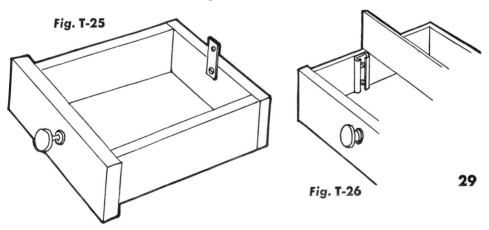

Fig. T-25

Fig. T-26

29

Here's an addition to a kitchen drawer that will save a lot of looking time. Put a few cup hooks inside to take care of those keys that you have to have but don't use very often. It also beats having a key ring that is too bulky.

Maybe the chest or desk top or sides are damaged. The same steps apply to warped or split tops as with tabletops. Many times the side panels will be loose, but some are intended to be. They fit in slots, and since they are not fastened in place, they can expand and contract as Mother Nature or your heating system dictates. A complete split can be glued back together, and this is best done with the panel removed. Both complete and partial splits are repaired in the same way as split tops. A coat of sealer inside will help prevent a recurrence.

Discarded wooden spools from the sewing basket can become low legs for chests. You can either slice off the top or use as is. Countersink a wood screw through the hole in the spool to attach it to the base of the furniture piece.

Chapter 4

Replacement Parts and Transplants

It may turn out to be impossible to just repair certain parts of the piece of furniture you are restoring. You may actually have to replace them.

In a later chapter, we will touch on some furniture you can make, but basically this isn't a book on furniture making. Certainly, from the sketchy information here, you'd be hard-pressed to produce any decent-looking furniture. However, as you progress in your fixin' phase, knowing about these components will be helpful.

Structural parts underneath aren't that much of a problem. But what about a knobby leg or spindly rung? Unless you have a lathe or are adept at wood carving, you will probably do well to have the part custom-made.

A cabinetmaker can do this in no time if he knows what you need. Usually, there are duplicate parts, and your best bet is to remove a duplicate and take it in to the cabinetmaker. He'll not only match the shape, but should match the wood. Another job usually for the pro is any part that has been bent by steam to shape. You might be able to do it, but probably you wouldn't have either the equipment or the knowledge.

There are some parts, however, that you can make without lathes and other equipment. Round chair rungs or spindles can be made from dowels. If the original is slightly tapered, you can duplicate this by hand-sanding or by using a rasp or surform tool and then sanding.

Larger roundish parts can be fashioned from an old hoe or rake handle. In fact, old tool handles are very good wood, and they are usually aged and will finish out more like the rest of the piece of furniture than a brand new dowel. Garden tools are usually made from ash, broom and mop handles mostly birch. Hammer handles, ax handles and the like are usually hickory.

Maybe the best source of replacement parts is to be found in broken-down old furniture—the kind that there is just no way to repair. Although a rung may not match the one you want to replace, it may be a lot easier to fashion it to match than to start from scratch. If you're going to do this furniture fix-and-finish bit seriously, you'll want to save any old parts you run across in Grandma's garage, the junk shops or wherever.

WOODS

What I'll try to tell you about woods will be just a splinter of what could be said. There are complete books written on the properties of *Sequoia sempervirens* (California Redwood) and *Juglans nigra* (American Walnut), plus all the other species. But it is good to touch base (or is that bass), on the woods used in furniture, because the properties of wood in some cases dictate what finishes you can use for best results.

You'll see the terms "softwood" and "hardwood" used frequently. If you have jumped to the conclusion that softwoods are soft and hardwoods are hard, jump back. Some softwoods are harder than some hardwoods, and vice versa. The classification is botanical and has nothing to do with their hardness. Softwoods come from coniferous or needle-bearing trees, like pines and firs. Hardwoods are from deciduous or broad-leaved trees.

The Wood Table (pun intended) gives you just the bare essentials (see Table III, pp. 34–35). Refer back to it when you get around to your first project.

If you want to know more about a particular species of wood, there are several that have their own associations you may write to for free literature.

Now that you're a wood expert, you should also become a lumber expert . . . or know how wood is graded and sold. Hardwood, softwood, and plywood each have a different grading system. "Who cares?" you may say. "All I want is to end up with a good-looking refinished product." True, but knowing what to ask for helps you get there at the lowest cost and with the fewest headaches.

Most of the lumber for cabinetwork should be kiln-dried. Specify this. Next, you can buy lumber either rough or surfaced. Unless you have the power equipment for surfacing, you'll want this step already done.

As to size, a one-by-four isn't one inch thick nor four inches wide. That's the size it was in the rough when first cut from the log. Removing the moisture shrinks it, and then when all sides are dressed or surfaced, this shaves off more. The table below shows what the yield should be according to the new standards set up back in 1970. You will be happy to know that if you order an eight-foot-long piece of wood, it will be at least eight feet long.

LUMBER SIZE TABLE

YOU ASK FOR: (Nominal Size) (Inches)	YOU GET: (Inches)	BOARD FEET Per Foot in Length
1 x 2	$\frac{3}{4}$ x $1\frac{1}{2}$	$\frac{1}{6}$
1 x 4	$\frac{3}{4}$ x $3\frac{1}{2}$	$\frac{1}{3}$
1 x 6	$\frac{3}{4}$ x $5\frac{1}{2}$	$\frac{1}{2}$
1 x 8	$\frac{3}{4}$ x $7\frac{1}{4}$	$\frac{2}{3}$
1 x 10	$\frac{3}{4}$ x $9\frac{1}{4}$	$\frac{5}{6}$
1 x 12	$\frac{3}{4}$ x $11\frac{1}{4}$	1
2 x 2	$1\frac{1}{2}$ x $1\frac{1}{2}$	$\frac{1}{3}$
2 x 4	$1\frac{1}{2}$ x $3\frac{1}{2}$	$\frac{2}{3}$
2 x 6	$1\frac{1}{2}$ x $5\frac{1}{2}$	1
2 x 8	$1\frac{1}{2}$ x $7\frac{1}{4}$	$1\frac{1}{3}$
2 x 10	$1\frac{1}{2}$ x $9\frac{1}{4}$	$1\frac{2}{3}$
2 x 12	$1\frac{1}{2}$ x $11\frac{1}{4}$	2
4 x 4	$3\frac{1}{2}$ x $3\frac{1}{2}$	$1\frac{1}{3}$

Table III
WOOD TABLE

Species	Uses	Freedom from Shrinkage & Swelling	Freedom from Warping
Ash	Tool handles, furniture, oars, baseball bats.	Medium	Medium
Basswood	Furniture parts, woodenware. (Can be disguised as other woods.)	Low	Medium
Beech	Furniture, flooring, woodenware.	Low	Low
Birch	Furniture, cabinet work, mill-work, dowels. (Can be made to look like cherry.)	Low	Medium
Cherry	Furniture, caskets.	Medium	High
Chestnut	Furniture, frames. (Often stained to look like walnut or oak.)	Medium	High
Elm	Veneers, furniture.	Low	Medium to low
Gumwood	Furniture (often stained to look like mahogany), veneers.	Low	Low
Mahogany	Furniture, veneers.	High	High
Maple	Flooring, woodenware, furniture.	Low	Medium
Oak	Furniture, floors, store fixtures.	Low	Medium
Pine	Furniture (often unfinished).	Medium to high	High
Poplar	Furniture (simulates other woods with staining).	Medium	Medium
Walnut	Gunstocks, paneling, fine furniture.	Medium to high	High

Hardness	Workability	Bending Strength	Filler Needed	Stain
Medium to high	Hard	High	Heavy	Yes or no
Low	Easy	Low	None	Always
High	Hard	High	Thin	Yes or no
High	Hard	High	Thin	Yes or no
Medium to high	Hard	High	Thin	Never
Medium	Medium	Low	Heavy	Yes or no
High	Hard	Medium	Heavy	Yes or no
Medium	Medium	Medium	Thin	Always
High	Medium to easy	High	Medium	Never
High	Hard	Medium to high	Thin	Never
High	Hard	High	Heavy	Yes or no
Low	Easy	Low	None	Always
Low	Easy	Medium	None	Always
High	Medium	High	Medium	Never

Hardwoods have standards. The National Hardwood Lumber Association got all their members to agree on a single system—which is more complicated than the following basic chart shows.

HARDWOOD LUMBER GRADES

First Grade	91⅔ percent of the total surface (both sides) is clear of defects.
Second Grade	83⅓ percent of the total surface (both sides) is clear of defects.
F. A. S. (Firsts and Seconds)	The above two grades are usually sold in combination.
Select	One side must be at least second grade, and the other must be #1 Common. (See below)
#1 Common	66⅔ percent of the total surface is clear of defects.
#2 Common	50 percent of the total surface is clear of defects.

Softwoods all have their own grading system. I know that's confusing, but it's a fact of lumber life. It goes a lot deeper than the following chart, but this will put you on the right track when buying. Always tell your lumber dealer what your project is, and he'll help you end up with the right stuff.

SAMPLE OF SOFTWOOD GRADING

(The grades are the same, but standards vary with different species—the standards below are for white pine.)	
B & Better Select (#1 and #2 clear) Supreme	Contains only minute blemishes. Suitable for all furniture work including tabletops.
C Select (Choice)	May have small sound knots or torn grain, but still suitable for most furniture uses.
D Select (Quality)	Larger imperfections, but still sound. Usually needs to be used on furniture to be painted.
#1 Common	Contains sound, tight knots and very few blemishes. Painted or rustic furniture only.

#2 Common	Slightly more pronounced flaws, but still acceptable for painted furniture.
#3 Common	Contains loose knots, as well as more pronounced flaws. Generally used where it won't show.
#4 Common	Bigger, looser knots, and even knotholes. Always used where it won't show.
#5 Common	All that's required is that the board holds together . . . so it's not for us furniture fixers.

Ordering plywood sheets is simple as far as sizes go. A four-by-eight foot sheet measures exactly four feet by eight feet. If you order ¾-inch plywood, it's ¾-inch thick. But you need to specify the species of wood you want on the face. Also, plywood comes in "interior" or "exterior" grades. The difference is in the glue. Exterior has completely waterproof adhesive.

Now all that's left is grading. The following chart for plywood doesn't get into all the different grades, but covers those you might use in furniture.

PLYWOOD GRADING FOR PANEL FACES

SYMBOL	DESCRIPTION
N	The best! N stands for natural finish. No flaws or defects.
A	Neatly made repairs make it usable for many furniture applications, and since N is often not plentiful, you may have to settle for A. Smooth and paintable.
B	Solid surface veneer in which tight knots and circular plugs are permitted.
C	Complicated formula allows for 1-inch to 1½-inch knotholes, providing total knothole widths fall within a certain limit. Also has limited splits. Use where it won't be seen.
C PLGD.	That's C-plugged. An improved C. Smaller splits, and knotholes limited to ¼″ x ½″. Still has to be hidden.
D	Knots and knotholes up to 2½ inches and even ½-inch larger with ratio limits. Strictly for out of sight.

(The inner plys on all interior plywood readily available are C or D . . . mostly D. Exterior plywoods generally have C-grade inner plys. Otherwise, the only difference is that the exterior type has 100 percent waterproof glue.)

Keep in mind that you're buying two surfaces. If only one side will ever be seen, it's not necessary to pay for a perfect veneer on both sides. In other words, an "N-D-int" would mean you'd get that perfect N on the face and a back with knots up to two and a half inches wide. The "int" means interior. Here again, tell the dealer what you're going to do; he may have some suggestions.

Unsightly plywood edges are covered with matching edge tape.

Before you go out looking for a square piece to make a replacement part from, check to see if you can rob something from the structural parts that are not going to be seen. The wood underneath may be the exact species and is certainly already aged to match. Then it's a mere question of whether you'll do better replacing the structural part or seeking another source for your replacement part.

SAWS

It's difficult for the furniture fixer to pick out one best all-around saw. It's certainly not going to be the carpenter's saw from your workshop. Once you know what each kind of saw is best for, you can pick out or borrow the right ones as needed.

Backsaws — They are so named because they have a stiff spine. The rigid back renders a very straight cut. These come in the several varieties shown in Figs. S-1, S-2, and S-3. The more teeth in a backsaw, the finer the cut. A backsaw is used in a miter box, which guides the saw in angular cuts used in joints. The miter box shown in Fig. S-4 is an inexpensive wooden job costing about a buck. It does fine unless you really get into lots of picture framing, when you can make better use of metal jobs costing over a hundred dollars.

The dovetail saw is smaller than the type used for miter boxes and has a thinner blade. Use it for cutting dovetails, pins, tenons, and doing other precision work. (These cuts are shown in the various joints in Chapter 5.) The razor saw has an even thinner blade and is used for super-precise small cuts . . . really more of a tool for furniture makers than for fixers.

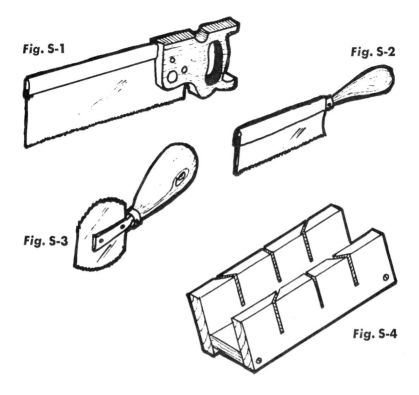

Fig. S-1

Fig. S-2

Fig. S-3

Fig. S-4

Hack saws — Made for metal cutting. They are good for cutting through bolts or screws that are frozen, and can also be used for straight, fine cuts when you don't have a backsaw.

Coping saws — For cutting very sharp turns and tricky shapes.

Keyhole saws — When you need to start cutting in the middle without an edge to start from, a small hole allows this pointed blade to get in and go to work. It can cut curves and make semi-sharp turns.

Veneer saws — Has a razor-thin blade for finest precision cuts required on veneer work, and can even be used against a metal straightedge.

Carpenter's saws — This saw will certainly come in handy for bigger sawing chores. The best all-rounder is a twenty-six–inch cross cut with eight teeth per inch.

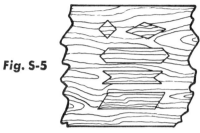

Fig. S-5

A broken-off corner or a gouged-out place in a top can often be replaced with a patch. As with veneer patches, match is important. If you determine that the first aid treatment of stick shellac or plastic wood won't do, but a patch is called for, you must then decide if it will be a complete plug or just a surface patch. Base your decision on looks first. Then if there's no difference, select the type that will be easiest for you to install.

For a gouge in the center of a flat surface, your best go is usually the surface patch. If the damage goes all the way through, or if it's on the edge, you're usually better off with a complete plug.

Either way, the shape is important. Right angles to the grain of the wood show up like a tattoo in a beauty contest. Lines with the grain blend in. To get around the sharp right angle to the cross grain, it is best to have about forty-five–degree angles at each end. I've shown several shapes that blend in fairly well when the grain of the patch runs with the grain of the wood. The actual shape you pick will be governed by the shape of the damaged spot (Fig. S-5).

After you figure out the proper shape that will completely cover the damaged area, make a template from a piece of shirt board. Lay this down over the botched-up place and draw a line around the template with a razor blade or sharp knife.

If it's to be a surface patch, you'll need to dig out the area marked off. This digging can be done with a chisel, pocket knife, or wood-carving tools.

Chisels The top of the list here are wood chisels. Buy a set of several and keep 'em sharp. Practice and you'll soon be able to do fine work with a chisel. Most precision work with chisels is done by hand force. Never use a hammer. A mallet can be used for some types of cutting.

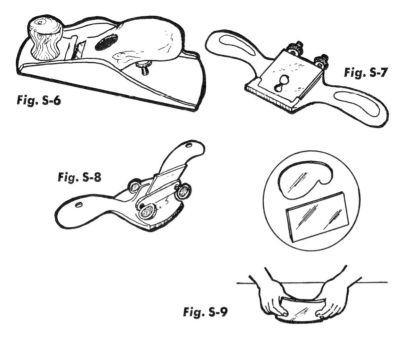

Fig. S-6

Fig. S-7

Fig. S-8

Fig. S-9

Carving tools A set of these will take up where their cousin, the chisel, leaves off.

Planes There are many sizes and varieties. A block plane (Fig. S-6) is a small one primarily designed for end grain cutting. The bigger planes, such as fore planes, jack planes, and smoothing planes are generally for carpentry work. Most of your furniture refurbishing won't call for any of these three bench planes.

Spokeshaves (Fig. S-7) This is a small sort of plane with a handle on each side. The two handles give you better control for curved surfaces. It comes with both curved and straight bottoms.

Cabinet scraper (Fig. S-8) As you can see, it looks like a spokeshave, only smaller, and is used on the final smoothing before sanding. Old-timers used a hand scraper at this stage. It's a thin tempered-steel blade either pushed or pulled and held at about a seventy-five–degree angle (Fig. S-9). The pressure of your thumbs forces the blade into a slight curve.

Rasps   These are actually wood files. Coarse shaping of wood is done quickly with a rasp. You can get one that is flat on one side and curved on the other, and with different teeth on either end for different cuts.

Surform tools   These relatively new shaping tools are really neat. These tools have replaceable cutting surfaces that have many tiny cutting teeth (Fig. S-10) that work like individual planes. Some look like planes, others like files. All are fun to use and do a good job of smoothing and shaping.

Fig. S-10

Knife   You'll find a pocketknife or hobby knife helpful lots of times.

Excavate deep enough to get below the damage. The sides of the hole should be straight up and down. The bottom can be rough, however, and in fact, will be a better gluing surface if it is. The patch should be a little thicker than the hole, but must be exact around the edges. (The reason you make the patch a tiny bit thicker than needed is so it can be sanded off even with the rest of the top.)

It requires a lot of patience to get the patch to fit exactly, but you can do it. In gluing the patch in place, put the goo on both the patch and the hole. Press it firmly in place, and then drag out the encyclopedias to be placed over waxed paper for weight.

If a complete plug in the middle of a flat surface is called for, you'll have to drill a hole through the damaged area big enough for a saber-saw blade to fit. If you don't have a saber saw, a keyhole saw will do. If the piece goes on the edge, just mark it off and saw away the bad parts.

A complete plug might fall on through the hole, so you will do well to screw a base of plywood to the bottom to hold the plug in place until the glue sets. If the patch is on the edge, it can be clamped in place by a bar clamp, tourniquet, or whatever seems right. An edge patch that is very big will be much more permanent if you'll go to the extra trouble to use dowels in the joint.

How easy or difficult the repairs are will depend on how bad off the furniture is to begin with. Let's hope you don't have to use anywhere near all the knowledge you gained in this chapter . . . but it's there just in case. If nothing else, it may give you enough of an insight into what's involved in a particular repair to know you don't want to tackle it. If not, go to a pro. Whether you do it or have it done, get the job done right. There's nothing worse than getting a beautiful finish on and have the whole thing collapse the first time you use it!

Chapter **5**

Veneers

The big expanse of tabletop generally is less likely to have problems if it's composed of several pieces joined edge to edge. However, you then sacrifice looks. Many times, the solution is to use veneer or plywood over large areas.

Veneers are paper-thin sheets of wood cut from round logs, of a kind of wood usually much more expensive than the frame, chosen because their grain gives a beauty hard to achieve in a solid piece. (Plywood, in most cases, is veneer over a core.) It can be applied over a less attractive piece of wood to give a super appearance for a lot less cost. In most cases, even a solid piece couldn't duplicate the look that can be had from really good veneers.

Because it is only a thin layer, it's subject to all sorts of problems. But because it's pretty, it's worth fixing.

Surface blemishes such as dents or scratches are covered in the next chapter.

Probably the most common veneer problem is the blister or bubble, caused when the glue beneath separates, leaving a space where moisture can get in. It's really a very localized warp. A small blister can often be pressed back in place with an electric iron. The heat will remove moisture from the wood and soften the glue underneath. Once the veneer has made

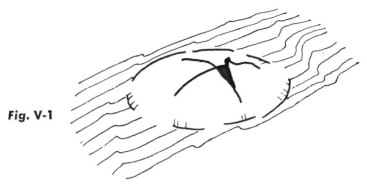

Fig. V-1

contact with the soft glue, all you need are a few volumes of the encyclopedia to hold it down until the glue sets up. (Incidentally, the iron should be only moderately warm, and there should be a dish towel or some such pad to protect the finish.)

That's the easy way—but it doesn't always work. Sometimes there's no glue left underneath or it's a kind that doesn't resoften. You'll need to get new glue in under the bubble—but the new glue may not adhere to the old glue, and so you'll need to clean out the cavity.

I think the best way to get at the cavity is to make a four-flap opening. Using a very sharp razor blade, make two slits across the blister to form an X as shown in Fig. V-1. If it's a fairly big blister, make only one slit, carefully following the grain of the wood. Try to keep any slits from cutting directly across the grain of the veneer—a lazy X may be better than one with strict right angles. Now you can lift up the flaps and scrape out the old glue. If the wood seems too brittle to allow you to lift the flap, dampen it. Clean both surfaces under the flap. If the dried glue scrapings leave a fine powder, be sure to remove this. A vacuum cleaner will suck it all out, or a damp Q-tip will pick it up. When clean and dry, insert glue and press down. Remove any adhesive that is squeezed out and cover the area with waxed paper. Then weight it down. Use first aid to disguise the surgical scars.

Some people completely cut out a patch of the old, brittle veneer. This gives easier access for cleaning and allows for pressing the patch down flat.

Although glues don't always adhere to one another, you can try injecting new glue into a blister. This calls for only a tiny hole instead of flaps. A regular glue injector or a hypodermic needle can be used. Here again, when the veneer is pressed down, some of the adhesive will ooze out the hole. Clean it, cover with waxed paper, and weight it down. If it doesn't hold, you may still have to resort to surgery, but you've only lost a little time and a little glue.

Veneer also has a habit of getting loose around the edges. If you get to it before dirt gets under the veneer, try the heat-and-weight-and-wait method first. Then try additional glue. Clean away the excess, weight it down—and hope. If dirt is under the veneer, you'll have to cut out a flap so you can clean it out.

You may find a place where the veneer is just chewed up or otherwise damaged so it has to be replaced. Replacing is easy, but finding the replacement may not be. You'll be looking for the same species of wood, the same shade (or one that can be stained to the same shade), plus a grain pattern that will match up. Just maybe you can steal a piece from some other area of the furniture where it won't show. However, since veneer is put there for show anyway, this usually won't work. Chances are you have to buy a sheet of the right veneer from which to cut your patch.

By rubbing a damp cloth across the bare veneer, you'll see what it will look like when finished. If it needs darkening, you'll have to stain. Unless you're going to refinish the entire piece of furniture, finish the veneer before you put it in place.

The replacement job starts with your cutting out the bad part. For you to be able to cut a patch to fit, the hole you cut out must have completely straight edges. A sharp razor blade and a metal rule are the only way to go. The cutout doesn't have to be square, but all sides, whether there are three or thirteen, must be straight. When the hole is cut, scrape away all the veneer fibers and the old glue. Now place a sheet of tracing paper over the hole and carefully trace its shape. Cut this out, and you have a pattern from which to cut your patch.

An alternate way is to cut out the patch first and use it as a pattern for the hole. (Incidentally, many veneer sheets are thin enough to be cut with a sharp pair of scissors.)

A section of veneer with several spots to be patched may be better being entirely replaced. Most likely you'll be able to

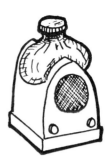

Fig. V-2

Ice pack filled with water conforms to and puts weight on odd shape. Warm water will help most glues set up quicker.

remove the old veneer without too much trouble. Sand or scrape the finish and cover the entire piece of veneer with a couple of layers of wet cloths. Many glues used in veneers are softened by vinegar. A half water, half vinegar solution may speed up the process. Keep the rags moist. After about ten hours, test the edges with a knife and see if it'll lift off. If it doesn't come loose, keep soaking. Save the old veneer. You'll find uses for it in future veneer patching.

An entire big piece needs pressure over the entire surface. A piece of plywood, large enough to cover the surface, will spread the weight of the set of encyclopedias.

Since gluing any laminate or veneer requires pressure over a wide area, here are a couple of stunts my readers suggest to get weight without getting a hernia. One placed a large washtub on the area that was glued. Then he used a hose and filled up the tub with water. When the job was done, he siphoned the water out. All he ever had to carry were the tub and the hose.

Another hint is to use bricks as weight. They will add up to as much weight as you need, but since they are individually easy to carry, you don't have to be Charles Atlas to make the scene. (Is he still around?)

A patch on a rounded surface also needs clamping. A hot-water bottle, ice pack, or sandbag with a tourniquet around it can solve this problem (Fig. V-2).

Applying Veneer — To apply new veneer to an old surface, you'll need to go over the entire surface with a fairly coarse sandpaper to give it "tooth" for the glue. Clean it off completely so there's no sanding dust left.

Sliced veneer leaves come in long narrow strips, while the rotary cut comes in big sheets. From an ease-of-installation standpoint, the bigger the piece the better. However, the effects obtained from butting matching grain patterns together is often worth the extra work.

If you're using strips, cut them out and lay them out just as they'll be glued down. This gives you a chance to arrange them in the most appealing way. Cut them the exact right size as to length, but allow about ½-inch overlap on all edges that are to butt against another strip.

Several glues work well for putting veneer in its place. Whatever kind you decide on, read the instructions and follow them. Until you get the hang of it, I'd suggest you steer clear of the contact types . . . 'cause when cemented surfaces touch, they can't be moved. That means there's no way to move it if you get it down slaunchways.

Okay, when you've got the glue on the first strip, put it in place. Rub the sheet down firmly against the surface. There are rollers made for this, or you can use a kitchen rolling pin. The next strip is placed so it overlaps the first by about ¾-inch. Take a *very* sharp knife—a utility knife will do—and a straightedge. Bear down hard enough to cut through both layers. Be sure the cut is right down the middle of the overlap. Remove the two snipped strips and roll over the seam. Roll from each side toward the seam. When the surface is completely covered, you need pressure until the glue sets. There are veneer presses, or you can use weight. Books are good, (Even if you don't like my books, they can be used to apply pressure to veneer during this step.)

Sometimes before you get around to putting veneers on, they sit around in the shop and become wavy. The waves will come out if you dampen both sides with a sponge and warm water. Then place the strips flat between boards until dry.

If you want to practice veneering on a small scale before tackling a big job, seek out a kit for small items like a serving tray, card table, or whatever you can find.

Once your patching is finished, chances are you'll want to refinish the entire surface to make the patches blend in—and that's what the next section is all about.

Part Two

FINISHING

Okay, now you've got this piece of furniture so it's sound, but you know you still want to do something to it. How do you want it to look? If it's a new unfinished piece, you know it's got to have something slapped on it. If it's old, you've got to decide whether it needs refinishing or just touching up. For the time being, let's forget about that new piece and see what the old one has going for it.

Chapter **6**

First Aid

Unless you've gone ape over refinishing, there are times when you can get away with just a little touch-up. If the furniture piece just has slight surface damage, at least try the touch-up route before going the whole nine yards.

Stick shellac is a beautiful way to take care of all sorts of surface problems such as burns, gouges, dents, and cracks. However, it requires a small amount of expertise . . . so play around with it before you start on an actual piece of furniture. Here again the key word is "patience."

The first thing to do is select a shellac stick that matches the finish of the piece. The better manufacturers put out a color chart, and there are dozens of shades available. (After you're an expert, you'll find the stuff can even be blended while it's flowing.)

From my mention of "flowing," you've probably already guessed that the stick has to be melted. The molten shellac is dripped into the hole, and then spread with any tool that has a blade like a pallet knife. Or grind the teeth off a piece of old hacksaw blade and fashion a handle as shown in Fig. FA-1. Even an old kitchen knife would do.

Fig. **FA-1**

Teeth of hacksaw
blade filed off

51

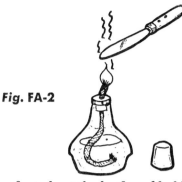

Fig. FA-2

Now back to melting. Some prefer to heat the knife and hold it to the stick. Others heat the end of the stick and let it drip. Some use a soldering iron, but the best heat is from an alcohol burner (Fig. FA-2). The flame is the right heat, and it won't leave any carbon on the blade as a gas flame does. However, if you have to use a flame that leaves carbon, wipe the blade on its way from the flame to the shellac.

As the molten shellac is smoothed into the wound, you'll have to reheat the blade to keep working the shellac into the hole. Build it up just a hair above the level of the surrounding surface. Heat the blade and smooth it over. Then let the spot cool and harden. Now it needs to be cut down even with the surface. The best way is to use a very fine abrasive on a sanding block with rubbing oil.

It may sound like a snap, but do take time for a little practice before you tackle the real thing.

You'll also find wax sticks in the paint stores. They are applied in much the same way: heat, drip, and smooth. However, this substance is not anywhere near as durable as stick shellac. Also, all of the smoothing has to be done with the blade, because sanding will just gum up the wax.

Here are a few injuries that require just a little first aid as opposed to surgery.

Scratches   Scratches that haven't penetrated the finish of the wood may need nothing more than a wax job. If the stain has been scraped away, you'll need to touch it up. There are wax sticks at the hardware store in all the various wood tones. Over the years, however, the very creative readers of my very creative column have come up with other scratch hiders.

A kid's crayon can hide a blemish, and chances are there's a color almost the same as the original stain. Crayons can actually be used as a substitute for wax sticks. With either, colors and shades can be mixed to reach the desired tone. After you've drawn along the scratch, rub in the wax with your finger, and then polish with a soft cloth. After the wax is smoothed, a coat of thin shellac is desirable before any finish is applied.

The several shades of shoe polish can get the job done. Apply this with a toothpick with a small amount of cotton rolled on the tip. *Don't* use this if the furniture piece has a dull finish because after you apply the polish you have to rub it dry with a soft cloth—and that makes it shine.

Nut meats can often be rubbed over a blemish and leave enough color to hide it. Break the nut meat in half. Eat one part and rub the other along the scratch.

Linseed oil will sometimes hide scratches. It's particularly good where there are a bunch of little scratches over a wide area. Some people use boiled linseed oil right out of the can. I prefer a mixture of two parts boiled linseed oil to one part turpentine. (Remember, boiled *does not* mean you put it on the stove and bring it to a boil. It means it's been treated with driers, and that's what you ask for at the paint or hardware store.) Whether you use it straight or mixed, rub it on with a lint-free cloth and wipe off any excess until it's dry to the touch.

Iodine will give first aid to some scratches. New iodine has a reddish-brown cast, while an older bottle may have turned dark brown. It can be diluted with denatured alcohol to lighten it.

Felt markers now come in lots of colors and can often hide a furniture zit.

Really big botches will have to be filled with stick shellac, wax stick, or plastic wood.

If there is a jerk around who strikes matches on a painted piece of furniture, there are two things to do: (1) Rub a lemon wedge across the mark to remove it, and (2) Break the culprit's arm as a gentle reminder not to do it again.

Burns   You first need to scrape away the charred part. A sharp knife, one with a curved blade, is best. As soon as you reach solid wood, stop scraping and smooth the spot with fine sandpaper or steel wool.

After cleaning away the debris, you'll have to decide whether it needs to be restained. Your hardware or paint dealer will probably have a small can of a stain that just matches. Or maybe you'll want to try one of the other touch-up tricks we'll discuss later. Next, you've probably got to fill in the gouge you made. Maybe it's shallow enough for paste wax to do the job. If not, you'll have to fill it with stick shellac or plastic wood. Stick shellac is probably the best way to go. If you don't have the patience to build up the burned hole, or if there are so many that touch-up seems unreal, consider sanding off the entire top and making it level again. Sometimes you may even find the flip side of the top can be finished, and you'll have a new surface for the smokers to go after.

White Spots   The boozers around the house always set glasses down, and the ice in the glass causes condensation on the outside, and water leaves a white ring or spot. Spilled alcohol or a hot coffee cup can also leave white spots. The best method is to rub carefully with the grain with a fine abrasive and some sort of lubricant.

You'll be surprised at what works as an abrasive. Naturally, a fine steel wool qualifies, as does powdered pumice and rotten-stone. But would you believe cigar ashes, table salt, or bathroom and sink scouring powder? Silver polish and combination cleaner and polish for cars may do the job too, since they both contain fine abrasives.

The potpourri of possible lubricants is even more startling. From machine oil and linseed oil, you can progress to olive oil, mayonnaise, lard, cooking oil, salad oil, petroleum jelly, and paste wax.

If you know the white spot is from water, you can often lift the spot with a blotter and a *warm* iron. Use a clean blotter and be sure the iron isn't hot. If there's no sign of the spot going away after several pressings, get on with the rubdown.

If you know it's an alcohol spot, and if you get right on it, just a whisper of household ammonia may sober it up. Take a barely damp cloth and add several slugs of ammonia, squeeze it as dry as possible, and brush the spot lightly with the rag. (Incidentally, booze isn't the only source of alcohol spots—perfume, shaving lotion, and some medicines contain alcohol.)

Fig. FA-3

Surface Dents   Among the worst surface mars are dents, proving you don't have to drink or smoke to mar furniture. Many times a wet pad and a hot iron will raise a dent. The principle is that the moisture penetrates the wood, causing it to swell, and thus removes the dent. Some folks just place a folded-over damp cloth on the wood and use a moderately hot iron. Keep it moving so you don't run the risk of the heat affecting the finish.

Another technique is to place a bottle cap between the iron and pad (Fig. FA-3). Just hold the iron steady and this concentrates the heat over the exact spot of the dent. Sometimes just holding a steam iron a couple of inches from the surface will allow the steam to do its thing. However, before trying either method, remove surface wax so the heat can get to the wood. If this doesn't work, it's the stick shellac drill.

General Grime and Dirt   Here you have to decide if the problem isn't simply a buildup of wax and oily polish. It probably is that, combined with greasy cooking fumes and the soil from just being around the family every day. Any of the combination furniture cleaning and polishing compounds will probably make it look new again.

If you're sure it's a varnished surface, the old-time way to clean it is with mild soap flakes in a quart of warm water to which three tablespoons of boiled linseed oil and one tablespoon of turpentine have been added. Wash with a rag and use a soft brush in any carved spots. Quickly wipe dry, and when it's had time to be completely dry, rewax or use furniture polish. Remember, however, that water can be bad for furniture—it's a natural enemy of wood.

Cracking and Checking   As discussed elsewhere, heat and humidity can cause this. As soon as it's noticed, apply paste wax with very fine steel wool. Rub gently with the grain and buff immediately.

Candle Wax Wax splatters are hard to remove without scratching up the surface. Holding an ice cube against the wax will make it more brittle. Try first to chip it up with your fingernails, and if that doesn't work, use a spatula. Another approach is the blotter and warm iron. Keep moving the blotter over so the iron doesn't remelt what the blotter has already lifted. Next time, get dripless candles—their drips are easier to clean up.

Feeding or Reviving — Sometimes, a varnish or shellac finish will be dull but otherwise in good shape. Rather than remove it, many restoration experts will go through a process called "feeding." (No, this doesn't mean smearing peanut butter over the finish!) The idea is to dissolve the very top layer but not remove it, so that the dirt and wax—foreign elements that cause the dullness and usually discoloration—are loosened.

The feeding of shellacked surfaces is easiest. The diet is prepared by adding a few drops of boiled linseed oil to very thin shellac. Dip a pad of superfine steel wool into this, and rub the surface with a light, quick stroke. Then go back over it with clean steel wool, very lightly, to remove the streaks.

The recipe for feeding varnish is two parts turpentine mixed with one part boiled linseed oil. Using the superfine steel wool pad, lightly go over the surface. Then take a dry, lint-free cloth and wipe with the grain to leave just a thin oily film. When dry, feed it again. It may take several such feedings to get it back to being a thing of beauty—but most diets take a while. During the drying period, protect the piece from lint as best you can. Many old-timers use raw linseed oil which takes a couple of weeks to dry. That means six feedings might blow an entire summer. If you've got the time, they swear it gives you a much better end result.

Another expert uses two parts varnish to two parts boiled linseed oil to one part turpentine. Use the same m.o. as above. I tried this and didn't like the results, but he swears by it.

Faster feeding can be done with prepared refinishing liquids that advertise they can refinish varnished, shellacked, or lacquered finishes without stripping, sanding, staining, and sealing. These usually have a base of methyl (wood) alcohol, acetone, or ether. The man who first introduced me to these preparations refers to them as "amalgamators," and I've since heard them called "reamalgamators." Still another expert calls the process "refusion," while others refer to it as "reviving." The good brands are expensive, but are fast and yield effective results.

Feeding is not going to work in every case, but it's certainly a less drastic method than refinishing. You've got to have a good solid finish on the furniture. Otherwise, the food dissolves all the way down beyond the finish and can upset whatever is underneath. Also, if the finish had a stain mixed with it, it'll be streaky. That means putting more solvent on and wiping away the old finish until it's all gone or at least until the streaks are gone. Then refinish over what's left when the surface is dry.

THE SUPER FINISHER'S PLATFORM

Unless you are a midget, you'll probably find it more convenient to have some sort of pedestal that raises the piece you're working on. This prevents an aching back and enables you to get at the lower parts of the piece more readily. A pair of sawhorses and a piece of ¾-inch plywood is ideal; it raises most chairs so you don't have to stoop, but can still reach the top.

For those of you who plan to get into this thing in a big way, build a platform as shown in Fig. FA-4. All of the pieces for the base are two-by-fours. The top is ¾-inch plywood.

After it's put together with wood screws, make certain it's level. Otherwise, all your reglued pieces may have a rakish look to them. Keep a scrap of old carpet around to cover the top when repairing a piece of furniture that must be turned on its side. Also, if you feel you might want to dismantle the platform between projects, use bolts and nuts rather than wood screws.

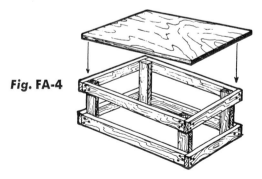

Fig. FA-4

Chapter 7

Stripping

Quickly, lest the book be X-rated because of the title of this section . . . it's about removing *finish*, not clothes.

First of all, what is your E. Q. (Energy Quotient)? How much work do you want to invest? If you're on the lazy side, keep in mind that an opaque finish such as paint will most likely go right on over the old finish. This means you won't have to strip, and this saves a ton of time. Paint also is a great cover-up for poor patch-ups, crummy crack fills, and other uncraftsmanlike conduct. At this point, both old and new furniture pieces should be examined to see what they need.

Don't strip the finish off guitars, violins, ukes, or mandolins. This often tends to deaden the sound box. (In my case, what could it hurt?) Instead, feed the finish, as discussed earlier. But if the finish that's on now is one you hate, certainly you'll want to put a new one on.

When the jury is in, and the verdict is "refinish" instead of "revive" the old finish, you usually have to start stripping —removing old finishes. At best, this is a messy job. The commercials that show a curvy young thing in a $150 sport outfit smiling as she brushes on "Super Strip," and then flash to her in a bikini hosing off the old finish, just ain't so. (At least not with the finishes I've run across—or is it that I don't have the figure for it?) However, it's not an impossible job.

Sanding and scraping are two surefire ways to remove almost any finish. But most of the time it's a long, slow process. There are basic, better ways to tackle the removal of shellac, lacquer, varnish, and paint.

The first step is to determine what the old finish is. That will tell you what methods to use.

Distinguishing among shellac, varnish, and lacquer is not easy for some of us. If you can't tell by looking, here's how to find out. First, since shellac will dissolve with its own solvent, it's easy to find out by applying denatured alcohol to a rag and dabbing and rubbing on a small wax-free spot. If it's shellac, the finish will start to get soft and rub off.

In a matter of seconds, the denatured alcohol goes to work on the shellac. It's best if you use a steel wool pad to liberally apply the liquid. Then follow with a rag to wipe away the glop. Since it evaporates rapidly, just work a small patch at a time. It does an even faster and better job if you'll mix in lacquer thinner with the alcohol—a ratio of about a cup of lacquer thinner to a quart of alky. Removing a shellac finish is done when you wipe away the glop—no rinsing, no neutralizing, no sanding because of raised grain. As soon as all the remover evaporates, in fact, you're ready for whatever your next step is, even putting on a new finish.

If the finish won't come loose with alcohol, it's either lacquer or varnish. So next, try the same routine but with lacquer thinner instead of denatured alcohol. If it's lacquer, it'll soften and start to come off. (Be sure to test for shellac first, because lacquer thinner also softens shellac.)

The procedure for lacquer removal is exactly the same as for shellac removal, except you substitute lacquer thinner for denatured alcohol. Again, mix a cup of denatured alcohol in with a quart of the base remover for better results.

If nothing happens with the lacquer thinner either, we know it's not lacquer. We've already proved it's not shellac, so what is it, class? "Varnish!"

But varnish is not going to be that easy to remove. It calls for one of the commercial paint and varnish removers, and the same things we're about to mention about paint apply here. (In fact, paint and varnish removers will also remove any other finish. However, that's the hard way on such easies as shellac.)

Probably the easiest finish to hang a name on is paint, but you really have to find out what *kind* of paint.

If the surface of the piece is to be covered with an opaque finish, you may not have to remove the old paint, but the old finish must be sound. If it is flaky or powdery, the new paint is not going to be any better. You do need to clean the old finish to remove any wax or dirt. Then you have to take off the gloss, because paint won't adhere to a glossy surface. This can be done with light sanding or with a commercial de-glosser. Also, you need to find out if there is a coat of shellac over the paint. In fact, on a piece with several layers of old paint, you may discover a layer of shellac somewhere down in there.

If there is shellac over the paint, you've already seen how easily it comes off. Once this is gone, you're ready to tackle the paint. And most of the other experts are going to tell you to remove the old finish . . . no matter what.

Lye — Old-time furniture fellers still use lye for stripping when there are many coats of paint on a piece of furniture. The fact that they're old should certainly relieve your mind a little on whether you'll be eaten alive. You could be devoured, and so could your furniture. But with proper use, lye does a good, safe, and very inexpensive job of removing even as many as five or six layers of old paint—even the bottom layer that's hard as rock from age. Where do you get lye? That's a good question: alongside all the fancy liquid drain uncloggers that the supermarket carries, they'll have a few cans of lye. If they don't, the hardware store or paint store may come through for you.

Here's how you can do it and still be around next week to refinish:

1. Do it outside—or on a concrete surface with drainage.
2. Select a spot where the runoff won't get on the lawn or other vegetation.
3. Pick a warm day . . . the warmer the temperature, the faster the lye eats.
4. Have the garden hose hooked up and ready, a bucket of water handy and a large bottle of vinegar. Vinegar, which is acid, acts as a neutralizer to lye, an alkaline.

5. Get into old clothes. At the least, have on a pair of rubber gloves, and if you have 'em, rubber boots.
6. Now you're ready to mix. Use a galvanized or porcelain bucket, because lye nibbles at aluminum and throws off poison gas. Use a big container so that there's no danger of sloshing over. Make a strong solution, or the lye will take too long to really soften *all* the paint, but will get through some of the paint and get into the furniture below.

   Always add the lye to the water. Never pour the water over the lye—and you don't need to mix or stir. You'll see the lye dissolve. One can (thirteen ounces) of lye to one quart of water is a good strong solution.

   (*Super hint*: If much of the surface is vertical, the lye solution will run off too fast. Add three or four tablespoons of wheat paste or cornstarch to one quart of lye to thicken the mixture.)
7. Now you're ready to smear on your remover. Use a disposable cloth mop with a wooden handle . . . an old dish mop for small jobs or a floor mop for bigger ones. Or make your own from a stick and an old pair of boxer shorts as shown in Fig. ST-1. Just mop it on.

Fig. ST-1

Note: If any lye gets on you or your clothing, don't panic, but don't dillydally. It doesn't start eating you instantly, but it will go to work shortly. Flush it off with lots and lots of water, followed by vinegar.
8. After only a couple of minutes, start checking with a scraper to see how deep the softening process is going. The size and shape of a scraper depends on the amount of goop that's to come off and the piece it's coming off of. In most cases, it's safer to use a putty knife than a scraper because you have better control and therefore less chance of damage to the wood.
9. As soon as you can start scraping off layers of paint, do so.

10. When you find it's down to the wood, turn the hose on moderately and bathe the entire surface. Now turn it up, and the water pressure will remove much of the paint that's left. A stiff wire brush may help get even more off.
11. When you've hosed, scraped, and brushed all that readily comes off, towel-dry the entire surface.
12. Now you need to brush on a generous coat of full-strength vinegar to neutralize any lye that's left. Many old time "lye-ers" use a second coat of vinegar after the first has dried.
13. During the vinegar period, you can continue to scrape any stubborn spots, brushing on a dab of vinegar as they're removed.
14. After the surface is fully dry, if there are still a few spots of old paint, use one of the commercial paint removers on the spots, or scrape them away.
15. If the lye was not removed quickly enough, the wood may have developed dark spots. Don't despair. Rub on household bleach or oxalic acid as described in the next chapter.

Heat also removes paint. There are electric paint removers on the market. You can rent them rather than buy them, but they still aren't as fast as running a propane torch over the surface. Either way, the idea is to heat the paint until it blisters and then scrape it off. It's harder work than chemical removal.

If you go the torch route, you can also end up with a pile of ashes. This usually happens after you've finished. There was one spot that got too hot and smoldered until you went in for lunch. Some people use heat on old painted surfaces where many layers are involved and where they prefer the fire hazard to lye.

Sometimes there are paints on antiques that even lye doesn't remove. It'll be the bottom layer, and this happens if that layer is a milk paint (also called refractory paint). The milk base made the paint into something like casein glue. They're usually dark colors. Plain old household ammonia right out of the bottle applied with coarse steel wool will do the job—not at first, but eventually. The ammonia fumes will just about knock your head off, so this is a chore best done outside. Also, ammonia is hard on the hands if left on too long, so it's best to wear rubber gloves. The M.O. here is to have the ammonia in a container in which you can dip the steel wool. Keep dipping and rubbing all over the paint. Keep it wet. Eventually (ten minutes or less) the paint will start to soften, and a little more vigorous scrubbing with the steel wool will remove it. The more stubborn spots may need scraping. When it's off, rinse with water and dry. Ammonia does darken the wood, so bleaching (next chapter) is in order.

Paint Remover — The best thing to use in my book (and this is my book), is a good brand of commercial paint remover. They come in liquid and paste. If it's for a horizontal surface, the liquid is fine and costs a little less. For vertical surfaces, however, the paste won't run out on you. The important thing about any of the dozens of good brands around is to *follow the directions*. If they give you a warning, heed it. If they tell you to clean the piece afterwards with a solvent, do it—even though it looks like all the old paint is gone, and the surface is ready for the new finish. The reason for the solvent is to remove all traces of wax, put in many removers to retard evaporation.

Here are a few pointers that may not be on the label: Use old brushes for application of liquid paint remover. I always keep a packet of cheapies around—throwaways from the dime store—for stripping and for solvents and removers. (For all other brushing, it's best to get the better brushes and to take good care of them.)

Use lots of old newspapers underneath. Brush only in one direction when putting it on. Going back over it disturbs the film that the wax forms to retard evaporation. If possible, do one horizontal surface completely. Then flip the piece over to work on a side while it too is horizontal. If you're doing legs, put them in tuna cans to catch the stripping liquid as it runs down (Fig. ST-2). Dip your brush into the cans so as not to waste the liquid. Check the time indicated on the label to see about how long it takes for this kind of stripper to do its thing. When that time has elapsed, see if the old goop has softened all the way down to the wood.

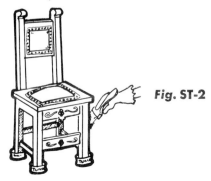

Fig. ST-2

Linseed oil finishes are removed with the commercial paint and varnish removers, following the same routine.

Wax finishes are dissolved by rubbing with turpentine or paint thinner. However, if the wax was worked into the pores of the wood, you may never get it out. If you're going to paint or varnish over it, the wax will prevent the paint from sticking. A coat of shellac will seal in the wax.

Another way of stripping surface coats down to the bare wood is with a block of silicon carbide in a solid foam form. I ran across it at the Chicago Do-It-Yourself Show where it was being demonstrated by a couple of Canadians, who called their product "Jack-the-Stripper." This stuff cuts through several old coats like magic, and leaves the wood fairly smooth. Only a little touch-up of superfine abrasive is needed before refinishing. Of course, this doesn't remove stains that have been absorbed into the wood—just any and everything on top. Hopefully, by the time this book is out, these guys will have distribution in your favorite hardware or paint store. If not, you could order a block direct. Send $1.25 to:

> Jack the Stripper
> 1373 Freeport Drive
> Mississauga, Ontario
> Canada

The only drawback is when the block is rubbed across any surface, it throws off an odor like rotten eggs. If you don't know about it ahead of time, it's a real surprise, but it only lasts for a few moments after you stop.

If the stripping process doesn't grab you, you may find a firm that specializes in furniture stripping. Most medium-sized cities will have one or two. They use whatever method is called for and return your furniture to you completely nude. Some of them have very creative names . . . like "The Strip Joint." Generally, they do a pretty good job, and if you want to avoid a messy part of refinishing, this may be the way to go. However, if their method is to dunk the piece in a vat of remover, that may also weaken or dissolve the glue. If you don't want to have your chair handed back to you in a basket, you'll do well to discuss this ahead of time.

Chapter **8**

Preparing the Surface

With all the major repairs made, and the old finish stripped away, you'd think it's about time to start slapping on a new finish. But the key to that perfect look when it's all done is in the proper preparation of the wood. *Now* it's time to prepare the surface. If it's wood—and that's what we talk most about in this book—in most cases that means sanding, staining, and sealing. This is a vital step and usually a true test of your patience.

Once again, a very close inspection is called for. Check for dents in the surface. If there are surface blemishes, check out the remedies under First Aid (Chapter 6). Also, particularly if you plan on a stain or clean finish, make an eagle-eyed inspection for any discolorations. The spots you find now will certainly show up through any transparant or semi-transparent finish. Even if you plan an opaque finish, the spot may prevent the covering from adhering to the wood.

Grease spots can usually be lifted by using spot remover intended for clothing. Follow the directions as to proper ventilation. After the liquid is wiped on over the spot, cover the damp part with sawdust or cornmeal. This dry stuff lifts out both grease and remover. If it didn't get it all out, try again. Other grease-spot removers are acetone or benzine. I don't have the foggiest notion why I happen to have both on hand, but most households won't. Fabric spot remover liquid is easier to come by, so that's probably your way to go.

Some unidentifiable spots will have to be bleached out. However, darkened areas back in the recesses may be desirable since they will add contrast to the finish. If it's a piece that should have an aged look, consider leaving the darkened areas. Always remember that if you don't like the way it looks when you're done, you can strip it all off and start over again!

Although some of the same principles that apply to bleaching out stains go for bleaching out wood color, this is strictly a spot approach. Most spots will come right out with a little liquid laundry bleach. Use it right out of the bottle, and rub it on with a rag or brush. The bleaching action begins immediately and is accomplished in minutes. After it's finished, wash the area with plain water. When dry, the spots should be gone.

Another bleach many people use is oxalic acid. Most paint stores carry it. The directions are on the container. It works best when applied hot and needs to stay on the spot for ten or fifteen minutes. Then it has to be neutralized with either vinegar or ammonia. The disadvantage to oxalic acid (beside the fact that you don't already have it on hand) is that it often shows where the spot was with a slightly different shade of wood. This usually means that you have to go over the entire surface to avoid replacing a dark spot with a lighter one.

Household ammonia will also remove spots. Wipe it on and allow it to dry. It needs no neutralizing, but often requires several doses to get the job done.

When stripped, the wood will sometimes have no spots, but will still have a sort of faded, dull, lifeless look. It first needs a bath with hot water and detergent. Scrub it off well, then rinse and wipe dry. Now here's where it'll pay you to track down that oxalic acid. While the piece is still wet, wipe on oxalic acid mixture and let it stand for about ten to fifteen minutes. Wash it off and neutralize with vinegar or ammonia. When dry, the life will be back in the wood in most cases.

BLEACHED BLONDES

While I'm not a fan of blond furniture, it is a fact of life. Also, there are times when wood is darker than you'd like it to be.

There are two ways to make it lighter: bleach it out, or color it lighter with light stains or whitish fillers.

We've already talked a little about bleaches. You'll recall that they actually remove some or all of the pigment from the wood. Regular old liquid laundry bleach will do it, as will household ammonia or hydrogen peroxide.

Preparation for bleaching includes *complete* cleaning of the piece. Remove the old finish, any dirt or grease, and all wax. Then, using fine steel wool, go lightly over the entire surface. The surface will now let the liquid penetrate and do its thing.

Laundry bleach can be used right out of the bottle. When it has lightened the wood enough, wash it off with plain water. If the first time around doesn't get it light enough, you can keep putting coats of bleach on until it gets there.

Oxalic acid, available in powdered form at most paint stores, is the wood bleach preferred by some. It's a mild acid, but it works a bit faster than laundry bleach.

Store-bought furniture bleaches are best because they are quick. However, you must carefully read and then follow the directions. They are so effective that if you leave them on a minute or so too long, you may have bleached out more than you wanted to. So if you just want to bleach a little out, the less effective laundry bleach may be a safer route to take.

Apply bleaches with a brush that has nylon bristles, or the stuff will eat up your brush. Shoot for as even a coat as possible. Uneven coats can give blotchy bleach jobs.

No matter what bleach you use, be careful. Even laundry bleaches can be dangerous. Avoid contact with the skin from any bleaches. If you goof, wash off as soon as possible.

After the bleaching is done, and you've neutralized the bleach, give it plenty of time to dry out completely. Incidentally, water neutralizes laundry bleach and oxalic acid. The store-bought jobs may require vinegar or something else, so be sure you find out and have what's needed on hand.

Undoubtedly, the grain will have been raised by the bleaching solution, so sanding will be necessary. If you like blond furniture, you've now got just enough information to get going on it.

Sanding — With all the spots gone, and the bruises taken care of, you're ready for the smoothing action. The final finished look will be governed to a large extent by the wood underneath. You can't expect the piece to look right if the wood has scratches or if it has fibers that stick up to give it a hairy look.

If you decide to speed things up by using a power sander for the rough work, here's how they stack up:

Rotary-disc sander   This is the kind that probably came as an attachment to your power drill. Don't ever use it on any piece of furniture except on edges—and even then, edges that don't matter too much.

Belt sander   Use only in the coarse stages when you're cutting down the thickness.

Should you have to resort to a power sander for a top that has square edges, you're liable to round off the corners. However, if you'll clamp a two-by-four against the edges, the sander can't round off anything but the scrap.

Orbital sander   Does a little finer work and is a big help for the early stages of a big flat area. Follow up with hand sanding.

Never use any kind of power sander on veneer or carvings. It'll send old, brittle veneer sailing across the room, and can chew off the nose of an oak cherub before you know it.

Hand sanders   Most of the real smoothing will be done by hand sanding. There are lots of sanding blocks that you can buy or improvise. The key, however, is to select the right abrasive. The charts that follow tell about coated abrasives (sandpapers), steel wool, and abrasive compounds.

Sanding takes on a logical sequence. You start with coarse abrasives and work your way through finer ones. By coarse, I don't mean start with the coarsest you have. Select a grit that will smooth out the flaws without scratching the wood. On an already smooth piece, this may be a fine grit. As soon as all the flaws in the wood are reduced to the depth of the cut made by the paper, it's time to move along to a finer grade paper.

COATED ABRASIVE (SANDPAPER) CHART

Abrasive	Backings* Available	Grades Readily Available	Characteristics and Broad Uses
Flint	Paper (A, C, and D weights)	Extra coarse through extra fine	Least expensive type. Doesn't last long. Ideal for paint removal or uses where paper clogs. Use, clog, and toss away.
Garnet	Paper (A, C, and D weights)	Very coarse through very fine	Costs a bit more, but lasts five times as long as flint. Smoothing, shaping, polishing, and finishing.
Aluminum Oxide	Paper (A, C, and D weights)	Very coarse through very fine	A synthetic that does a great job for hand or power sanding including end-grain sanding. Is sold under various trade names.
	Cloth (X)	Very coarse through fine	For belt sanders
Silicon Carbide	Waterproof paper (A weight)	Very coarse through superfine	Also sold under trade names. Used for smoothing, shaping, polishing, and finishing.
Emery	Cloth (X and J weights)	Very coarse through fine	Only fine grades used in furniture work, largely for smoothing turnings.

* Paper Backing comes in A—finishing paper, most flexible; C and D—for cabinet work; and E—machine sanding. Cloth backing comes in J—for hand work; and X—for power sanding.

STEEL WOOL CHART

GRADE	USES
0000 (superfine) 000 (extra fine)	For super high finish in rubbing down after final sanding on shellac, varnish, or lacquer
00 (fine) 0 (medium fine)	General smoothing and for dulling gloss of linseed oil finish
1 (medium)	Paint removal
2 (medium coarse) 3 (coarse)	Not for furniture refinishing—won't smooth, but can mar the wood

Preparing the Surface **69**

The coarseness of sandpaper is designated in one of the three ways shown. This table compares each and shows the general usage you'll find for each in furniture finishing.

Grit	0 Symbols	Simplified Markings	Uses
600	none	Superfine	High polishing on all woods and for
500	none		satinizing shellac, varnish, and
400	10/0	Extra fine	lacquer top coats.
360	none		
320	9/0		
280	8/0	Very fine	Finish sanding undercoats and top
240	7/0		coats of paint. Final sanding
220	6/0		bare hardwoods.
180	00000	Fine	Final sanding bare softwoods and for
150	0000		smoothing a previously painted surface.
120	000	Medium	General cabinetwork and preliminary
100	00		sanding of bare wood. Preliminary
80	0		smoothing of previously painted wood.
60	½	Coarse	Rough sanding and paint removal.
50	1		
40	1½		
36	2	Very coarse	Very little use to the furniture
30	2½		refinisher—for extremely rough
24	3		shaping and for rust removal on
20	3½	Extra	cast iron furniture.
16	4	coarse	
12	4½		

Don't mess with coarse paper at all on edges and ends. Use only fine paper followed by fine steel wool. A sanding block is a must here to keep the edge or end square.

Sanding blocks are very advantageous. They give you a better grip and give the paper a more even backing. Curved surfaces need curved blocks. You can really go creative in coming up with the right block for unusual surfaces.

Always sand with the grain, never across it. Also, use even pressure and straight strokes. Try to give each area about the same number of strokes.

Clean the paper whenever it starts to clog. Tapping the sanding block against the floor will knock most of the sawdust particles out. A stiff brush is sometimes needed when sanding certain woods.

Between sandings, always clean the surface. Before the last few sandings, moisten the surface. Just rub it with a damp rag or sponge. When it is dry, you'll see little whiskers from the raised grain.

Turned and knobby surfaces also work out better if only the finer abrasives are used—paper, then steel wool. But sand in the direction of the turning instead of trying to go with the grain.

When trying to get steel wool small enough to smooth the small slits in turned legs, try the trick of twisting the steel wool around a piece of string. This makes it almost like a string of the abrasive and will do the job.

When you have reached a fine grit and the finish isn't being affected by the sanding, you're through—as far as paper is concerned. If you want an even smoother finish, you can use a superfine steel wool.

When you're all done completely, clean the surface. After the dust has been removed, then go over the entire piece with your tack rag.

Tack Rags — Many times throughout the book we'll mention a tack rag, and it's a tool you must have to remove dust from a surface. You can buy one at the paint or hardware store, but it's easy to make your own. Use a much laundered lint-free cotton cloth. First dip the cloth in warm water and wring it out. Next saturate it in turpentine and wring it out again. Now dip varnish all over the cloth and fold and squeeze until the varnish seems to be spread uniformly all over the cloth's surface. It should be tacky enough to pick up dust but not wet enough to leave any varnish behind. Keep your tack rag stored in a sealed glass jar. When it gets dry, revive it with drips of water and turp.

DISTRESSING TECHNIQUES AND OTHER CRIMES

Along about Christmas-time one year, I met a man who had written a book on antiques. I assumed he might be a dealer or a decorator and was delighted to learn he had a furniture repair shop. "Actually, it's a front," he confided. "In the back room, we make antiques."

We all had a good laugh, but when I visited the shop, they had several brand-spanking-new pieces that were beginning to look two hundred years old.

I'm not going to take you that far into aging, but will try to give you some tricks that will help add an antique flavor to some of your work without putting it in need of repair.

Wormholes For some reason, these are accepted as a sign of age. However, a properly protected old piece won't have any wormholes and a fairly new one could. Simulated wormholes are made by the splatterdashing techniques described later, under Painting. But the best wormholes are made with a *sharp* ice pick. Because it is tapered, the point leaves different sized holes as it's stabbed in at different depths.

Tiny twist drill bits can also be used, and we heard about a doctor who has some sort of pneumatic hypodermic needle for his wormholes. His patients have complained, but his waiting room and home are loaded with great-looking furniture.

As for a pattern of wormholes, you need to put yourself in the worm's shoes. (This is a figure of speech, as they mostly wear boots.) They would enter through one leg usually and come out in an area directly above that leg. Maybe there'd be enough of a colony to use two legs. There might be a few adventurous worms for scattered random holes.

Wear and Tear The surest tip-off that a piece of furniture isn't all that old is if it still has sharp corners and edges. Almost instant wear is given these areas with either a rasp or surform tool. Since wear won't be even, don't make yours that way. Also remember that rungs and cross pieces should show wear. When all the corners and edges are gone, you need to give surface areas that lived-on look. Here the most authentic-looking evidence of use is in the form of dents. The key is to vary the size and shape of the dents. Some experts whip their furniture with chains, and others beat it with a ball peen hammer. The best way is to use several different objects and don't get too carried away. A few dents here, a few there! It's a great way to relieve tensions . . . and if you're really up-tight, try punching it out with your fists.

Charring   A propane torch does a beautiful job because it can darken wood much as Mother Nature would over a hundred years. The softer parts char more, and are thus darker. With a little practice, you can learn to darken corners so they look like authentic aging. Don't let the torch linger too long or the fire department may come out and distress your house and furniture with a fire ax. A fine abrasive should be used before staining.

You remember in the stripping section we warned you about leaving lye on too long. Well, if you wanted darkened wood, leave it on too long. However, the best rule of char is still, "carry a torch"!

If you like the way the wood looks, you're home free; if not, there are ways to jazz it up. The use of the right stain will bring out the grain and color. In some cases, the stain adds color to an otherwise drab wood . . . and that's what the next chapter is about.

Chapter 9

Staining and Sealing

Let's assume you'll do whatever it takes. Then the first consideration is your taste. What do you want . . . colors or wood tones?

The next consideration—which may alter the first—is the wood. Does it have an attractive grain pattern? Is it possible to ever make it have an attractive pattern? Is it all patched up or does it need to be? Even though you might like to go for wood tones, if the piece has an ugly grain pattern or will look like a patched-up apple crate, it may need the hiding power of paint.

If the signs point to the natural look, you must then decide on whether the wood has enough going for it to use a clear finish.

SEEING INTO THE FUTURE

If you're down to the bare wood and plan on a clear finish, you'd like to know just how much change the finish will make. Will the grain be pronounced enough? Will the color change? By rubbing a damp sponge over the dry wood, you'll see almost exactly how the wood is going to look. This wet test will let you know whether it would look better with a little oil or stain before you spend all afternoon putting the clear finish on.

A friend saw me use the wet test and cringed. He's a professional stripper (of furniture) and his motto is "Never let furniture go near the water." He gets the same look into the future by rubbing a rag dipped in turp across the bare wood. (Incidentally, he's the kind of furniture stripper who does *not* hand your piece back to you in a bucket, so maybe his aversion to water has merit.) Water does raise the grain . . . but sanding is good exercise.

If the wet test showed the natural grain and color somewhat less than exciting, it doesn't have to be painted. Usually a stain can be applied to bring out its beauty.

Stains soak in and add color, but allow the grain pattern to show through. Some woods have no beauty, but a stain can be applied to make them look like something they aren't, helping an inexpensive wood take on the mask of a more expensive species. Stains can bring out the grain or hide it. They can accentuate color, push it into the background, or revitalize a faded wood. (Pine, poplar, basswood, and gumwood have little color and generally are stained. Other woods are so light-colored they just cry for stain.) Also, when the maker or repairer has used several different kinds of wood, a stain can make the piece look more uniform in color.

A look at the wood chart (Chapter 4) will tell you what woods are nearly always stained, those that are rarely stained, and those in between. Actually, that doesn't mean much if you've got an "always stain" chair that happens to have an interesting look during the wet test. It's a guide, but you're the judge!

You should be aware that the type of wood affects the way the stain looks. Stain from a single can will give you twelve different colors on twelve different woods. Also, just because it's a walnut stain doesn't necessarily mean you can put it on a piece of pine and make it look like walnut.

There are two basic breeds of stains: pigmented and dye stains. In spite of the fact that there are lots of stains you can buy or make, you can get most staining chores taken care of if you know about water stains, spirit stains, NGR stains, and pigmented wiping stains. The first three are dyes, and the latter is, obviously, tinted with pigments.

Although I give general directions for using various compounds, different brands may have slightly different components. The new miracle ingredient may require slightly different handling. So *read the directions* on the label. (Of course, all those people who never read directions until something goes wrong have probably skipped over this paragraph, too.)

Water Stains — In this type stain, powders are dissolved in water. Water stains are inexpensive since the powders are sold in small packets and mixed with tap water. They also result in good strong colors and have a wider variety of shades and colors than other types.

The disadvantages are that they are slow to dry, and they raise the grain of the wood, leaving it sort of fuzzy. Some finishers wet the wood with clear water and let it dry. This raises the grain, which is then sanded off smooth, so when the water stain is applied, it raises little or no grain.

Apply water stain with a wide, fairly stiff-bristled brush (I like nylon). Brush with the grain and always work against a wet edge. Overlapping a partially dried area will render a darker color.

Spirit Stains — In this stain powders of a different kind are dissolved in denatured alcohol (although some powdered dyes can be dissolved in water as well). Their advantage and biggest disadvantage is the same—fast drying. Fast drying isn't a disadvantage once you become an expert, but until then, you're liable to get lap marks and streaks. There aren't as many different colors available, and spirit stains aren't as permanent as the water stains. On the positive side, however, alcohol doesn't raise the wood grain.

I suggest you try this stain on small objects to avoid the problems of overlapping a dry edge. Therefore, you need a small brush. However, if you're going to go against my suggestion and try a big area, get a wide brush and work rapidly with the grain. Work right to the wet edge, but try not to overlap. Don't work back and forth, because each trip of the brush darkens the wood.

NGR Stains — The initials for non-grain-raising. These stains contain a chemical base that doesn't raise wood grain. They are mixed when you buy them, but can be thinned to adjust the color. Use the recommended thinner or denatured alcohol.

The same general rules we just mentioned in connection with spirit stains apply here.

Pigmented Wiping Stains — Here is a so-called stain that's really more of a paint. Color is added to a vehicle in the form of pigments that do not actually dissolve, but are just suspended in the liquid. They are quite popular because they are easy to use, easy to correct, and every paint and varnish maker puts out a full line of wiping stains. In fact, if you go in and ask for a stain, chances are this is what you'll get—even though it may not be right for your wood.

Application is brush on, wait a few minutes, and wipe off. You don't have to be careful about putting it on—just make sure you've got everything covered. Waiting and wiping are a little more important. You wait until the surface loses the wet look and starts to dull. Then you wipe with an absorbent cloth, trying to remove all the stain that will come off.

If you've tested the stain color beforehand on an obscure part, you'll know whether it's right or not. However, if it turns out to be too light, you can go back over with a darker stain. (Sometimes you can even go back over with the same stain, but leave it on longer before wiping.) Also, darker pigment can be added to the old mix before it's applied again.

Even if it's too dark, you can still correct it. Dampen your wiping rag with paint thinner and wipe some more.

"Okay, so we know about the types of stains. Where do I use what?" That's a good question. Actually, any stain can be used on any kind of wood. Generally, though, some stains work better on certain woods.

We've already learned that some woods are good-looking enough so that they don't need stain; also, most veneers don't need any. These woods include maple, teak, mahogany, cherry, walnut, and a few others. Sometimes, however, they may require just a little additional tone. If so, a water stain, spirit stain, or NGR are good bets. The water stain will be easier to dilute to get just the tone you want.

The close grained, usually light-colored woods may look better to you if they're darkened. These include oak, ash, beech, birch, Philippine mahogany, and the like. The same three stains are effective here as mentioned in the previous paragraph. Since lightness and subtlety of tone isn't as big a deal, I'd lean to NGR stains here.

Those woods that nearly always need help are pine, poplar, basswood, fir, spruce, and gumwood. They will take very kindly to the pigmented wiping stains. The pigment stays only where it's trapped, and these woods are porous and trap lots of color.

Most walnut stain is made without using a single walnut. Maple stain has no maple syrup. But tobacco stain is actually made from tobacco. It's a pretty doggone good stain that you can make for practically nothing.

A big problem with most city dwellers is in buying chewing tobacco. That's for hillbillies, hicks, and $75,000-a-year major league pitchers. Go on in and buy a plug. If you're wearing shoes, the clerk will just figure you're a ball player.

To make your stain, you don't have to chew the tobacco. (However, if you bought two plugs, try it.) Crumble up the plugs in the bottom of a quart mayonnaise jar. Pour in a pint of household ammonia, tightly cap the jar, and let it sit for about ten days. Now take the jar outside and uncap it. When you first uncork it, the fumes will take your head off, so leave it out for several house to let it sort of deodorize.

Now you got yourself some of my old granddaddy's tobacco stain. Before applying it, you need to strain it to get the tobacco bits out. Dampen the surface with a sponge and warm water, and then wipe on the tobacco juice generously. The warm water helps give the stain a more even distribution. Wipe off the excess.

Give it at least a day to dry, and then rub it lightly with 000 steel wool.

There may be better stains, but none will be as good a conversation piece. You can even claim it's some old formula from your own granddaddy, and according to the Surgeon General it isn't hazardous to your health. The finish you decide on will tend to darken tobacco stain just a bit.

Lightening With Stains — Most of us think of stains as darkening the woods, but they can lighten too if they have white pigment in them. They are pigmented wiping stains, so you brush them on, let them penetrate, and wipe 'em off. The preparation of the wood is the same as with the pigmented wiping stains already discussed.

BRUSHES

Brushes are naturally a must if you are going to finish furniture. Bristles are the key to a better brush.

While split ends are bad with hair, they're essential in bristles. The bristles with split, frayed tips are best, and this condition is referred to as being "flagged." Figure B-1 shows a single magnified bristle. On a good brush, the bristles are also tapered. Some brushes have natural bristles, while others have synthetics. You'll find advocates for both kinds, and you'll find good brushes in both categories. Generally, good natural bristle brushes seem to have the edge except for use with latex materials. The synthetics don't absorb the water in latex, but naturals do, and this causes them to lose their resiliency.

Of the naturals, China hog bristle gets my nod as being a sight better than the others.

Once you spend the extra loot for a good brush, you can get your money's worth by taking care of it.

The most important rule in brush care is to always clean the brush as soon as possible after using it. The same liquid you use as thinner will act as the solvent for brush cleaning. Read the label. In case you've lost the label, the chart on page 80 shows generally what to use.

Whether you belong to the wet or dry storage school, the important thing is to make sure the bristles are not ruined. If the brush is suspended, the bristles mustn't touch anything. If the brush is wrapped in paper, shape the bristles ahead of time.

A little loving kindness will make the good brush serve you for a long, long time.

Fig. B-1

BRUSH-CLEANING SOLVENT CHART

After Brush Used In . . .	Clean With . . .
Shellac	Denatured alcohol
Lacquer	Lacquer thinner
Synthetic varnish	Thinner recommended on can (If unknown, try turpentine or mineral spirits)
Varnish	Turpentine or mineral spirits
Paints, oil base	Paint thinner, turpentine, or mineral spirits
Paints, latex	Soap or detergent in warm water
Oil stains	Kerosene, naphtha, or turpentine
Spirit stains	Denatured alcohol
Water stains	Soap or detergent in warm water
Paste wood filler	Mineral spirits
Paint and varnish remover	Denatured alcohol

(Note: If the solvent suggested doesn't do the job, experiment with another. The best solvent will always be the one suggested on the label.)

HINTS ABOUT STAINING IN GENERAL

1. Be sure all the surface preparation is done. If you missed any blemishes, the stain will make them stand out, so clean the wood before you start. Wax, dirt, peanut butter, or whatever will prevent the stain from being able to penetrate the wood.
2. Test the stain. If you have an obscure part of the piece or a scrap of the wood, try out the stain to see what it'll look like. It's better, easier, and smarter to make adjustments before the stain goes on.
3. Particularly check the end grain areas. They absorb differently—usually more thirstily—than the flat areas and may require a different tone so as to ultimately blend with the rest. They may also require a wash coat of sanding sealer or a very thin coat of shellac.
4. If you're using pigmented stains, stir them well and often. Otherwise, the pigments settle and the stain loses some of its color.
5. Try to move the piece, if possible, so your staining is done on horizontal areas.

6. Avoid puddles, drips, splatters, trickles, and dribbles. They will be darker than the rest of the piece when dry. After the stain is on, additional sanding may remove the stain.
7. If you have to work on a large vertical area with a water stain, start at the bottom and work up. Any stain that runs down will go on an already stained area and must be wiped up immediately. With an NGR or spirit stain, start at the top and work down.

SEALERS

Now that the piece is stained, in many cases you'll need a sealer. It acts as a filler, which means less of the finishing material will be required. It can also give the finishing material a sounder surface to adhere to, and prevents any bleeding on the part of the stain when the finish is applied.

If you used a pigmented wiping stain, check the label. It may have had a sealer in it. If so, you won't need an additional sealer.

There are sanding sealers on the market, or you can use very thin shellac. (Be sure the finish you plan on can go over shellac. Some synthetics won't.)

Some people will use two sealer coats just to be sure. Unless you are using a prepared sealer that specifies two coats, one is enough. To assure that the final finish will adhere, follow the sealer coat with light sanding with 6/0 sandpaper.

FILLERS

Some woods have pores that need to be closed up or filled. If not filled, these pores hinder your getting a super smooth finish. To get a glasslike finish on open-pored woods such as oak, ash, mahogany, walnut, hickory, and rosewood, a heavy paste filler is probably needed.

Close-grained woods can often be finished without a filler. The finish coats themselves will level and hide the pores. At most, these woods should be treated with a liquid filler. Often a sanding sealer will do, although a liquid filler does have solids that a sealer does not.

If the wood is one of those no-character woods like pine, poplar, and fir, you'll probably not need any kind of filler. If you are going to use a penetrating resin finish (which you'll learn about in the next chapter) you want the pores open, so a filler is not called for.

Paste fillers come either colored or neutral. Neutral fillers are tinted by your adding the pigments to suit your needs. Colored fillers can be intermixed to get the right color. Generally, you'll want to come up with a filler just a shade darker than the stain—or wood color, if no stain was used.

In buying a paste filler, look at the ingredients on the can, and if one contains a silex powder base and another doesn't, opt for silex. It's better.

The instructions are on the label. It will need to be thinned, so check to see that you have a supply of the recommended thinner. If they don't specify, then turpentine, benzine, or paint thinner will do. The best consistency is about like heavy cream—thin enough to brush on, but thick enough to fill in the pores and not shrink in drying due to evaporation.

After it sets up, I use a piece of burlap rubbed across the grain to remove the bulk of the surface filler. Then I use a soft cloth, rubbing with the grain, to get all the rest off the surface.

Paste filler on carved surfaces can be removed with a stiff brush.

LIGHTENING WITH FILLERS

When we talk about using a paste-type wood filler, we suggest a filler slightly darker than the existing stain—or wood, if no stain was used. If the filler is lighter, however, this lightens the wood. On open-pored woods, you can do considerable lightening this way. You will want to apply a thin shellac wash coat so the light filler goes in the pores but doesn't lighten the surface.

Don't let the filler dry too hard before taking it off the surface, or it will become like concrete and must be softened to remove it. Most are set and ready to remove as soon as the surface luster begins to go. Liquid fillers are just brushed on like any coating.

Finally, the piece is ready for finishing. Now, that's doesn't sound too grisly, does it?

Chapter 10

Finishing Basics

After the piece is stained and sealed, or you've decided it doesn't need a stain, you're ready to decide on the actual finish. The finish is the protective coating that also brings out the beauty.

You can opt for either a surface finish or a penetrating finish. Your E. Q. (remember, Energy Quotient?) again enters the picture. In fact, many of the new penetrating finishes have stain, sealer, and finish all in one. What could be easier? Some surface finishes require several coats with work in between each coat.

Another factor is the use and abuse the furniture will be subjected to. Shellac is quick and easy, but a bar top couldn't have shellac because the first time you spilled booze, the shellac would dissolve. In fact, even a wet glass could leave a ring.

Consider also the type of look you want the finish to impart. How glossy do you want it to be?

I'll tell you what steps are involved in the application of each finish. You can then decide which one fits your E. Q. I'll try to describe the results that can be attained and tell you about the resistance qualities so you can apply all the factors against the considerations we've brought up.

The finish you decide on can even be a combination of finishes . . . and after it's done you may even come in with a coat of wax to protect the protective coating. At any rate, deciding on the proper things to do to a piece of furniture is just about as important as knowing how to do them. It means the difference between whether it is finished . . . or done for!

What do you need to get started? The first thing you needed was this book.

The next thing you need is a place to work. It doesn't have to be big. One refinishing buff (or is that buffing refinisher?) I know does all his work in an apartment kitchen, using a metal utility table as his workbench. But it does have to be warm, because every liquid you'll use—adhesives, finishes, and solvents—do better in warmth. (Most of us work better in warmth too.)

There should be plenty of light. You have to see what you're doing and what the finish is going to look like. And opt for a spot with clean air . . . dust, lint, and flying bugs can louse up a finish you've worked days to achieve.

Lastly, have a way to ventilate the work area when you're using volatile concoctions. Their fumes can give you brain damage or worse if you inhale them in any concentration.

If you have central heat or air conditioning, cut it off while finishing. It stirs up a lot of dust that you can't see . . . until it lands on the wet surface you've been working on so diligently. Any fan that moves air should be stopped until the finish is dry.

It's great, of course, if you have a place where the mess you make won't make any difference. Short of that, shoot for an area that's easy to clean. If neither type place is available, save your newspapers and be careful. (Plastic coffee-can lids are great to use under furniture legs when applying finish. The legs won't stick to them like they do to newspapers.)

Now you're ready to put the actual finish on the wood. We've already told you there are two families of finishes: penetrating and surface. The original penetrating sealer was the hard-rubbed oil finish. Those of the modern version are the penetrating resin sealers. Surface finishes include shellac, varnish, and lacquer.

Hand-rubbed oil finishing   One reason almost nobody does

this may be in the saying my old granddaddy had. His M.O. for oil rubs was, "Rub once a day for a week. Then once a week for a month. Then once a month for a year, and then once a year forever."

If stroking wood with a rag is your stroke, all that rubbing is not going to bother you, and you do get a deep, beautiful finish—eventually. Also, you get a finish resistant to almost everything.

The way my old granddaddy did it was to use a mixture of two parts boiled linseed oil to one part turpentine.

The mixture works best when warm. However, *do not* heat over a flame or coil. It's flammable. The safe way is to place the container of mixture in a pan of hot water removed from the stove.

The surface should be smooth and clean and wiped with a tack rag before the warm oil is applied. Rub it on generously with a soft lint-free cloth. Keep applying and rubbing until the surface seems to be unable to absorb any more of the mixture. Now wipe away the surface oil, wringing out the liquid as you go. You may do even better with a new cloth for this. It's important to get all surface oil off. When it's done, take a polish cloth to the surface for about ten or fifteen minutes or until your arm falls off. Then it's "every day for a week, every week for a month, every month for a year, and every year forever" with the same process.

Lots of folks have rediscovered tung oil as a replacement for linseed oil. I say "rediscovered" because it was used in China many centuries ago. It has advantages over linseed oil because tung doesn't darken with age as linseed often does. It's better in humid areas because it doesn't mildew as linseed sometimes does.

The disadvantage is that tung oil solidifies when exposed to air—even the little bit of air in the bottle when only one-fourth of the liquid has been used. Since tung oil is a bit expensive, this hurts. The key to conservation is to add marbles to the bottle each time you use it to keep the level at the top so not much air stays in with the tung oil. A hand-rubbed tung oil finish is applied just like putting on a coat of linseed oil. When the coat is rubbed in, let it dry for four hours in full sunlight if it's a warm summer day. Otherwise, let it dry overnight in the house and keep the room temperature at about 72° or more. This renders a no-sheen finish. If you want more luster, put on a second coat the next day. A third coat will give a high gloss.

The newer penetrating resin finishes are super easy. You simply brush on, wait for however long it says to on the label, and wipe off the excess.

If that sounds simple, it's because it is. There are only a few things to keep in mind:

1. Make sure *all* the old varnish, shellac, or lacquer has been removed.
2. Follow the directions. Some of these need only a few minutes to penetrate. Others may require a half hour.
3. Shoot for having the surface horizontal when possible.
4. Take care not to miss any spots and try for a generous enough coat to soak in well.
5. Don't jump the gun on the second coat. If it says to wait twenty-four hours, do it.

Usually two coats is all you'll need. Some makers suggest light sanding, but in most cases unless some of the grain has been raised, it doesn't make much difference.

As mentioned in a previous chapter, penetrating resin sealers also come with stains mixed in them. They can go over other stains. Although they can't go over an old surface finish, they can go over an old penetrating resin sealer.

Since there's practically no surface film, this finish doesn't scratch easily. It's also fairly resistant to spills. When something does goof it up, chances are you can blend in a touch-up without having to redo the whole piece.

If there isn't enough of a mirror finish, a good furniture wax will add that.

Now if you like the ease of the penetrating resin sealer, but would like to fake out a neighbor who is of the hand-rubbed oil finish school, here's how to counterfeit one. After the easy penetrating resin sealer has been on for a week, wipe warm boiled linseed oil all over the piece. Rub it in and wipe it off. It will almost have the look, feel, and smell of the "once a day for a week, etc."

Of the on-the-surface finishes, shellac is the easiest to apply, and is also easy to polish to a high degree of shine. Shellac is used in various consistencies. The consistency is described in terms of "cut." A medium-thick shellac would be a two-pound cut. That means two pounds of dry shellac resin is dissolved in one gallon of denatured alcohol. A three-pound cut is three pounds of dry shellac resin dissolved in a gallon of alcohol, and so forth, but only very few stores carry dry shellac. You buy it in either three pounds, four pounds, or five pounds already dissolved. Then you mix according to the table below to get the consistency you want. Accuracy isn't really that important—but if a one and a half pound cut gives you a super job, it's good to know for future use exactly how you did it.

SHELLAC CONSISTENCY CHART

YOU WANT	YOU HAVE					
	3-pound cut you mix:		4-pound cut you mix:		5-pound cut you mix:	
	Parts shellac	Parts alcohol	Parts shellac	Parts alcohol	Parts shellac	Parts alcohol
½ pound	1	4	1	5	1	7
1 pound	3	4	1	3	1	2
1½ pound	4	3	2½	3	1	1½
2 pound	5	2	4	3	1	1
2½ pound	5	1	2	1	3	2
3 pound	you got it	0	4	1	2	1
4 pound	—	—	you're in	0	4	1

Shellac comes in orange and white. The white is just orange that they've bleached out. White is used more often and dries clear. Orange shellac gives an amber look and is good for an antique effect.

When you buy shellac, don't buy more than you'll use for

an immediate project. It has a limited shelf life, and after about six months it's no good at all—it will never really dry. That also suggests that you buy a fast-moving, well-known brand from a volume dealer. Most good paint and hardware dealers don't keep a big enough stock for it to go bad. If you want to test some leftover shellac, brush it on a wood scrap, and if it's good it'll dry rock-hard and clear. If it's the least bit tacky or turns dark, throw it away and invest in a new batch.

The biggest disadvantage to shellac as a finish is its lack of resistance to water and alcohol. Water turns it cloudy, and alcohol dissolves it. In fact, even damp air can have an effect on shellac, turning it cloudy. Therefore, it just won't hack it as a finish for coffee tables, dining tables, bar tops, or any place where it's going to be subjected to liquids. A good coat of wax over the shellac is usually enough protection against humidity, but not against spills.

You should know ahead of time that a good shellac finish requires several coats. However, since shellac dries fast, this doesn't mean a week-long job. One suggestion is that you don't apply shellac in very humid weather or it won't dry very fast.

Clean the prepared surface with a tack rag. For the first coat, use a very thin coat (one-pound cut). Don't shake it in mixing, because that makes bubbles. Just stir it up. Put it on with a well-loaded, soft-bristled, fairly good-sized brush and don't dillydally because shellac dries fast. The fewer strokes the better, so develop a long, with-the-grain motion that flows the shellac on. Work fast, but don't stroke fast or you'll make bubbles. Make sure there aren't any skips by overlapping each previous stroke.

The first coat is usually dry in an hour or two, and needs smoothing before the next coat goes on. You can use either a coated abrasive or steel wool. Open-coated garnet, aluminum oxide, or silicon carbide paper (6/0–220 grit) is good. It's very fine, slow to clog, and can be cleaned with alcohol to be used again. A flint paper would do, but couldn't be used again, and would disintegrate besides, leaving bits of grit on your finish. 000 steel wool is my choice if you go that route.

The second coat goes on after careful dusting. You can use the same cut or a cut thicker. Subsequent coats will take maybe an hour longer to dry since there's no longer bare wood underneath to help absorb the alcohol. Therefore, a thicker cut helps to compensate.

When dry, it's smooth-up time again, but now with a lighter sanding. Some people move up the fineness scale of abrasives with each coat. In other words, a 220-grit after the first coat, 240 after the second, and so on.

The consensus is that you should use from three to six coats of shellac. After you've gained a little experience, it's a matter of personal taste. If the surface is to receive wear and tear, more coats add more strength.

Before applying the last coat, use a 0000 steel wool or a powdered FFF pumice stone and rubbing oil for smoothing. If the latter is used, you can rub the surface with cornstarch to make sure all the oil is removed.

After the last coat, some people leave it as is. Others will give it another fine smoothing to achieve a satin finish. Here again the powdered pumice and oil do the finest job.

If you're going to wax, wait at least twenty-four hours after the final coat.

French polishing is a method of using shellac for finishing and also for developing a strong arm. If used as the complete finish, this process can turn into a life's work. However, French polishing is also a great way to obtain a very high gloss on a finish or to patch without completely refinishing.

If you're going to use this technique as the complete finish, you put a layer on each day until it builds up to where you just can't stand any more delight. For this you start with a quick rubdown with boiled linseed oil over the smoothed, cleaned, and stained surface. Wipe all the surface oil off and let it dry completely.

If you're just going to use it as a polish, use the same technique over a shellacked finish.

When using it to repair a marred shellac finish, you just keep building up the surface of the mar until it builds up level with the rest of the surface.

Now for the technique. First, you need a pad. The outside cover needs to be of clean, lint-free cotton or linen that is freshly laundered. Use about three or four layers six to eight inches square. A man's old handkerchief folded twice is perfect. Now make a blob of cheesecloth or gauze for the core as

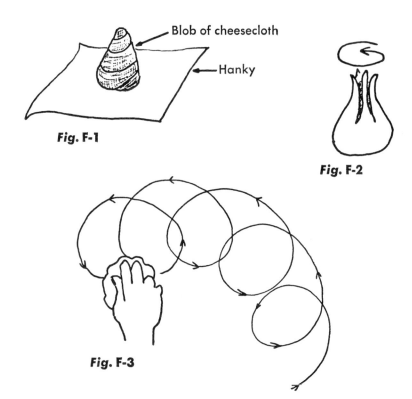

Blob of cheesecloth

Hanky

Fig. F-1

Fig. F-2

Fig. F-3

shown in Fig. F-1. Pick up the edges and twist around as shown in Fig. F-2. You are now ready to rub and rub and rub.

First, you pour shellac (I'd suggest one-pound cut) into a saucer. Dip the pad into the shellac and then squeeze it out. You want the pad to be wet but not dripping. Now you need a few drops of boiled linseed oil in the center of the pad. I keep a screw-on cap with a hole punched in it to replace the regular cap on the can of oil. This allows me to shake the drops out.

Before the pad touches the surface, you need to start your motion. Fig. F-3 shows you the action. Those circles are about six to eight inches in diameter. You'll be rubbing fairly fast and fairly hard. A little practice beforehand is a must to get the feel. When the pad runs out of shellac, keep the pad in motion even as you let up and remove it. Remoisten the pad, sprinkle on more oil, and start the motion. If it starts to drag as you rub, add a few more drops of oil.

The big thing to remember is *never stop moving the pad*

while it's in contact with the surface. Even a momentary stop will leave the pad's impression. So as Goldie Hawn used to say on *Laugh-In,* "Keep it moving!"

When you finally get the finish to the luster you had in mind, you'll want to remove any traces of oil. Also all that circular motion leaves some traces. Usually a clean, dry, soft rag will buff away marks and remove the oil. If not, a clean rag with just a whisper of denatured alcohol rubbed very quickly and very lightly with the grain will remove both oil and marks. Remember, this alcohol dissolves, so don't overdo it.

Chapter 11

Varnish and Lacquer

VARNISH

The most widely used of the surface finishes—although not necessarily the most popular—is varnish. The reason it's so widely used is because it provides a great finish that looks beautiful and is tough as a boot. It resists damage from water, alcohol, and heat, and is not that easy to get scratched up.

The reason for its lack of popularity is because it seems to fight you every step of the way. It attracts dust. In a vacuum, a fresh coat of varnish would somehow acquire a few flecks of dust to bug you. It's difficult to apply, and if you're not careful, you end up with brush marks or bubbles. Worst of all, it's slow-drying.

But don't let these problems scare you away from varnish. Be aware of them and learn how to avoid them. Without varnish, you are nowhere in the furniture finish game.

There are many types of varnish. The new ones use synthetic resins and help you to minimize the pitfalls we discussed above. The old oil resin varnishes do a good job, but have all the problems in full intensity. So it would seem a shame not to opt for a synthetic. Not only are they easier to work with, but most give an even more durable and equally beautiful finish.

"So which synthetic do I buy, Mr. Expert?"

Well, it's really sort of dealer's choice. There are vinyls that are super-quick drying but don't quite measure up to the alkyds or urethanes in the high-luster department. Alkyds are a little less expensive than urethanes or vinyls, but have a long drying time. Alkyds may not be quite as clear as urethanes or vinyls, but more so than phenolics. Urethanes can usually be had in glossy, semi-gloss, satin, and even flat finish. Vinyls and alkyds are usually available in glossy and satin; phenolics mainly in glossy only.

So, like I said back there, it's dealer's choice. They're all good, and you'll have to decide which best suits you. The only no-no is spar varnish for inside furniture. It's for outside use only. Whatever you decide on, read the directions, because different ingredients may require different treatments.

Here are some general steps to follow in applying varnish. First of all, the place in which you varnish is important. It should be as dust-free as possible, free from drafts, and yet have some ventilation. The temperature should be between 70° and 80°.

After you're all set up, dust the piece, vacuum the room, and then go sack out for a couple of hours so any airborne dust can settle.

The clothes you wear must be clean and lint-free. Synthetics are better than cottons or woolens. Actually, stripping yourself as well as the furniture is a good idea, because most nude bodies are completely lint-free. However, keep some clothes handy in case of unexpected callers.

The brush is important too. It's got to be 100 percent clean. Even a new brush should be worked to remove any loose bristles.

Just before you start to apply the varnish, go over the furniture with your tack rag.

Most people prefer to thin the first varnish coat just a bit. Use the thinner recommended on the label. Don't shake to mix—stir slowly so as not to create bubbles, and if possible, let sit for a while after stirring.

When you dip the brush into the varnish, don't make waves. Now comes the point where many varnishers disagree— striking the brush to remove the excess varnish. Some wipe the brush gently against the side of the rim. Others put a striker wire across the top. Some don't wipe but tap sharply against

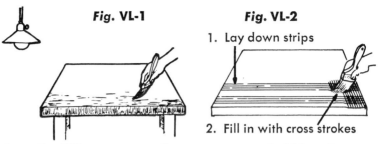

Fig. VL-1

Fig. VL-2

1. Lay down strips

2. Fill in with cross strokes

the side. Whatever you do creates some bubbles. I use a separate can right next to the varnish as a striker. This way, the bubbles go into this can. When I'm through, I pour the bubbles into the leftover varnish. Whatever way you decide on, the idea is to create the fewest possible bubbles.

When you brush it on, arrange to stand on a side facing a light or window. The reflection on the wet varnish will let you avoid skips. Whenever possible, have the surface horizontal (Fig. VL-1).

There are several schools about laying the varnish on. The main thing to remember is don't use a lot of strokes. The best way for me has been to first apply it in strips with the grain. However, leave a space between strips as putting the next strip against a wet edge will leave a brush mark. Then use as few cross strokes as possible to fill in between the strips (Fig. VL-2). Then draw the brush across the bubble can to dry it, and tip off with the grain.

Done right, you probably won't leave any brush marks, but if you do, don't fuss with them. They'll most likely level out. More brushing simply invites more brush marks.

If it's the final varnish coat and there are still brush marks, I usually take some very fine steel wool and dip it in lemon oil. Then I start giving the surface a gentle rubdown. The brush marks will seem to melt away . . . usually.

Don't try to do too big an area before filling in with the next. If the old area starts to set up before the new is connected, it leaves a ridge.

Avoid letting your brush fall off over an edge. The edge will act as a striker and leave excess varnish at the edge. The brush should be picked up at the exact moment the bristles reach the edge. Sounds difficult, but really it just takes a little practice.

Round things, such as legs and rungs, are best varnished by

first laying on the varnish around the curve and then smoothing lengthwise.

Now after you're through, you don't just stand around and watch the dust specks build up. You're going to fight back with a pick-up stick. This is a toothpick or match with a blob of sticky rosin on the head. Add powdered rosin to a few drops of varnish. Indirect heat will help dissolve the powder. When you've added enough rosin so it's stiff, dip the stick in. A blob will stick to the tip. When it cools, it will be tacky. By barely touching the tip to a speck and lifting straight up, the speck will come up too. (The rosin I use is the stuff I use for the bow of my musical saw. The musical kind or pitcher's rosin from the sports store will do.)

Loose brush bristles are also a pain. I try to use the tips of two toothpicks, like miniature chopsticks, to remove them. If you get them off quickly, the marks will level out.

After a successful first coat, the biggest mistake most people make is in not letting the varnish dry completely. There are some special formulas that should be recoated within a few hours. The label will clue you on these special cases. But otherwise, the best second coat is not put on for two full days. Some people won't attempt it until three days have passed. In humid weather, you may have to add a day. To be sure it's hard, push your thumbnail into an obscure part of the finish, and it should leave no impression. If it does, even if you've waited two days, wait some more.

Before going to the next coat, sanding is needed to smooth the surface and take off the gloss for better adhesion. Use either a 6/0 garnet paper or 0000 steel wool. Dust well and go over the surface with your tack rag before putting on the next coat.

Usually two or three coats of varnish are all that is needed. When you decide you've put the last coat on, it needs to be polished with a very fine paper or with pumice and oil as described earlier in this chapter.

LACQUER

The other surface finish is lacquer. This is used a lot more by manufacturers than by the do-it-yourselfer. They use it because it dries so fast. We *don't* for the same reason—it dries so fast that it's difficult to brush on properly. So if you don't have the spraying equipment or don't know how to use it, you run into trouble.

Lacquer is also incompatible to some things underneath. It acts as a solvent to many paints, and is not going to stop some stains from bleeding through without a sealer.

If you are going to brush on a lacquer, be sure you get brushing lacquer. It is slower-drying than spraying lacquer. (You could spray a brushing lacquer, but not vice versa.)

The newer lacquers are getting easier to work with, so maybe you'll decide to try them. If there's any doubt about whether the lacquer will attack the undercoats, play safe with a sealer coat of shellac.

Brushing lacquer is already thinned, but often needs additional thinners for the proper flow. Always use the thinner recommended on the label. Other thinners may make it thinner, but may also cut down on the quality of the eventual finish.

I find the wider the brush (within reason), the faster—and thus smoother the lacquer. Flow the lacquer on by keeping the brush as full as possible. Always work against a wet edge, with the grain, using a long single stroke—none of that brushing back and forth.

In just minutes, most brushing lacquers will be dry enough not to gather dust. It can be dry enough for another coat in from one to four hours. The label will tell you how long to wait between coats. Making sure the previous coat is fully dry is almost as important as getting it on properly.

Spraying lacquer should be handled according to the instructions on the can, plus the instructions that came with your spray rig.

Sanding between coats depends on how the previous coat looks. It's not needed for adhesion because the solvent in the next coat tends to dissolve the cover of the previous layer, bonding the two together. If there are uneven places, however, use a fine paper or steel wool. Be sure to dust and use your tack rag before the next coat.

After the final coat, wait a couple of days and then give it the pumice and oil rub.

Aerosol spray lacquers are good for very small projects, but would be costly for anything very large. They lay on a very thin coat, so a number of coats are usually desired.

Maybe the best advice I can give the amateur lacquerer is to use it only on small items or on pieces with lots of small areas. You don't run the risk of it getting tacky before you finish, so that way, the super-fast drying is an advantage instead of a problem.

And so that finishes our chapter on finishes! Next comes good old paint.

Chapter 12

Painting, Striping, and Stenciling

Those of the Transparent Coated School look down their noses at painted furniture. "If you can't see the grain, it might as well be plastic," a transparent coater once said.

Hogwash! The accents gained by colors can perk up any room if used right. Bold, bright colors are a must with some styles of decor. Besides what the colors can do, there are other good reasons for painting. It's easier, it hides better, it's quicker, and it's easier to clean. Best of all, it's easier to do over again next season.

Also, not all woods are created equal. Some woods just don't have a pretty grain. To let the ugly grain pattern show through would be like 230-pound Aunt Minnie wearing a bikini. Some things are better left unseen.

What color you decide on is up to you, of course. There are hundreds to choose from. Also, you alone can decide whether you want a glossy or a dull finish. On the far side of glossy are the new "wet-look" finishes that are extra glossy, very large in contemporary settings, and extra big with the young adults —even the ones only young at heart.

Different paint companies give their finishes different names. What is "semi-gloss" to one manufacturer may be "satin finish" to another. Only the sample will tell for sure. It will also show you the color the paint will be when dry. Be sure to check the sample under light conditions similar to those where the furniture will be. Both finish and color can look different under the fluorescent lights of the store than in the indirect lighting of your den. And of course there's no reason to check the paint in natural daylight if it's never going to be *seen* in the light from a nearby window.

Enamels are the most often-used paints for furniture. They can be brushed or sprayed on. Either way requires only a little know-how and a little practice.

For either brushing or spraying, the preparation of the wood is the same. The surface should be smooth if you want the repainted surface to be smooth. Even if you're not removing the old paint, sand it to make sure it's smooth and to remove any gloss. Next make certain the sanding dust is cleaned away by using your tack rag.

If you're brushing on the enamel, use a soft-bristled brush. Apply the paint to horizontal surfaces if possible, so you don't have to worry about runs and sags. This isn't always possible, of course. If you do see a run starting, touch it up immediately, and it'll smooth out. In applying, don't bear down, just flow the paint on. Any pronounced brush marks can usually be done away with by a light cross stroke using only the very tip of the brush. Don't get carried away and overbrush.

The small cans of paint used for furniture jobs are an easy handful. But when the paint dribbles over the side, it gets on your hands, spills, and generally makes a mess. You can add a handle to the can by using an old coffee mug. Slip the can into the mug, and you're all set. (Don't start daydreaming or you're liable to take a sip.)

I always try to think positively: "One coat will do it." It doesn't always work out that way, but often does. A second coat will add durability if that's needed.

If additional coats are called for, be sure to allow ample drying time for the previous coat. Then give a light sanding and clean the dust away.

Unfinished furniture paints better it is has a sealer coat. Dilute shellac with denatured alcohol—half and half—and brush it on. When it dries, smooth lightly with 000 steel wool.

A coat of enamel underbody is also recommended. It's white, so if you have a dark top coat in mind, tint the underbody. Either use a tint from a tube or mix one part of the finish enamel to three parts of enamel undercoat. Incidentally, this is so highly pigmented that it's difficult to spread. Try to spread it out completely or you'll end up with gummy spots. Let it dry for at least twenty-four hours before you lightly sand away any brush marks. Clean the dust away and you're ready to paint.

Spraying enamels is done either with a sprayer unit or with paint that comes in an aerosol can. All spraying units are different, and the people who make them put complete instructions in with the rig. Read them. If you rent a unit, find out how to operate it before you lug it home. An aerosol can will have instructions on the can.

Spraying gives you the fastest, smoothest finish . . . if it's done right. The biggest causes for not doing it right are (1) not reading the instructions, (2) not keeping the spray the proper distance from the work, (3) not keeping the gun or can moving.

Also, there are certain hazards to spraying. Overspray can get on things beyond the work. There's nothing worse than a $6,000 automobile that has a fine mist of cerulean blue all over one side of its once snow-white finish. Enamel fumes and vapor are toxic and in some cases highly explosive. A paint booth, proper ventilation, and a complete knowledge of how to use the equipment can take away the hazards.

After you're sure of what you're doing, here are a few tips to get a better-finished job:

1. Remove doors, drawers, and leaves.
2. Begin spraying horizontal surfaces at the edge closest to you and work your way across to the far edge.
3. Start the spray with the gun or can either in motion or not aimed directly at the surface.

If you do much painting with aerosol cans, save the little plastic nozzles of the type that slip off. Store them in a little jar of solvent. Since most are interchangeable, you'll never have to quit spraying when the nozzle you're using clogs up. (Also, when you're through, turn the can upside down and push the button until no more paint comes out. This clears the opening so it won't clog with dry paint.)

While you're thinking sprays, it might be well for me to mention colored lacquers. They're available in aerosol cans, are very quick drying, render a high gloss and a very durable finish. Most brands suggest spraying on several light coats to achieve the desired coverage.

As with anything in an aerosol can, if you've got much to cover, it gets quite expensive. But for a chair, small chest, or end table, you can spray it and put it to use almost immediately—and without the brush-cleaning chores. Maybe the difference in paint cost will be offset because you didn't have to use a solvent.

STRIPING

In addition to fixing up old standbys, there are all sorts of plain and unfinished furniture pieces that can become unique decorative happenings with a minimum of effort.

Striping generally refers to the fine lines that are painted about an inch or so from the edge of a piece. Even if you're the type who can't draw a straight line, you may be able to draw a stripe. In fact, the lining on a professionally striped piece may look straight, but being hand-drawn, it will have slight wavers.

The first must-do is to clean the surface. Use a compatible cleaner and be sure all wax is removed. However, you can do stripe painting on a surface sealed with a coat of shellac. Then if you goof, you can wipe off all traces and goof it up again.

Use a thinned oil base paint. Enamel is best. Use whatever thinner is recommended on the label in a ratio of about two tablespoons of thinner to a cup of paint.

The first secret is a special striping brush, which is usually short-handled with saber-shaped bristles. The second secret is don't try it out on the morning after the annual Beaver Club stag and smoker.

Key three is to always use a finger guide. A wooden yardstick usually makes a good one. Often the furniture edge can be used as a guide. Most stripers place the last three fingers along the guide, but some use only the last two. Fig. P-1 shows the

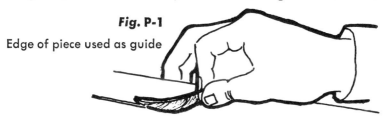

Fig. P-1

Edge of piece used as guide

way to use a guide and to hold the brush. You can see the brush is almost horizontal. The brush is always pulled toward you, and the best stripers only move with one continuous line.

A curved stripe needs a curved guide. Cut one from ¼-inch plywood unless you have something that is already the right shape.

The best approach is to have a practice area, and each time after you dip the brush, you take a practice stroke until the paint flows just right and leaves the perfect stripe. Now move over and lay down the stripe for real.

STENCILED DESIGNS

Stenciling and painting designs can give furniture the peasant look or the Pennsylvania Dutch treatment. These methods can also make the furniture look like you turned a class of first graders loose with a brush and paints.

Look through the various home magazines until you find some pictures of several pieces decorated this way. This will give you a feel for color contrasts, positioning, frequency of spots, and relative size. You'll also see how the designs have all been simplified.

An art store will have stencil paper and possibly even some already-cut stencil designs. They may even have a book on stencil cutting, and it will probably have some designs you can adapt.

Whatever design you decide on, you'll need to cut a separate stencil for each color. Try out the stencil on a practice surface to be sure it's what you have in mind. A shellacked poster board of about the same color as the furniture piece is a good testing ground.

The stencil is taped to the surface and the paint is daubed on with a stencil brush. This is a short, stiff-bristled affair that looks sort of like an old shaving brush. After the brush is dipped in the paint, it needs to be blotted on a paper towel to remove excess paint. Application is a matter of practice, but be sure you avoid working toward the stencil edge or you'll brush paint under it. Also avoid smearing the color already put down when subsequent stencil cutouts are put in place. This often means waiting for each color to dry.

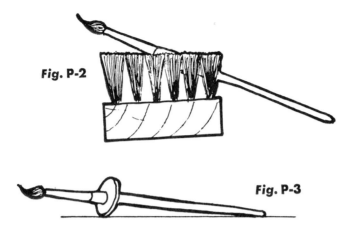

Fig. P-2

Fig. P-3

After all the stenciling is done, touch-ups or additional detail can be applied with an artist's brush.

Those small brushes used for decorations of furniture can be held up off the surface while not in use by wedging the handle in between the bristles of a scrub brush (Fig. P-2).

Another small brush-freak slips a tiny washer up over the handle until it wedges there. This gives the brush a rest that aims the bristles up (Fig. P-3).

PAINTED DECORATIONS

Hand-painted decorations accomplish much the same thing that stenciling does, but have a character all their own. However, this won't come off if you don't have a little something going for you in the talent department—not a big talent, but the ability to copy a simple style. Here again, find some painted decor you like and practice. If you've got that, then get artist's oil colors and artist's brushes—both pointed and square-end.

Thin the oils and use driers and then practice making your drawings with as few strokes as possible. After you've got it down, put it down on the furniture. Give at least twenty-four hours to dry. Then you can glaze or put a clear finish over it.

Chapter **13**

Antiquing

This is a very "in" thing—the term given to the application of a glaze over painted furniture. The fad started with the many antiquing kits that came on the market. You could take any piece of furniture, old or new, and by following the instructions on the kit you'd end up with a fairly neat-looking piece of furniture with a lot of character.

While the kit is the easy way, you can save yourself a lot of loot by buying just the components instead of the handy kit. For the base coat, any semi-gloss enamel will do. Latex is easiest to clean up after.

Next you need a glaze. Most paint and hardware dealers carry glazes in a wide variety of shades and colors. Actually, you can mix and make your own glazes. Oil colors, thinned with turpentine, can be mixed with a clear sealer. You'll need to stir it in well.

Keep in mind that any glaze will look a lot lighter after it's applied and wiped off than it does when mixed. The key to getting it right is to experiment. While painting on the base coat, also paint it on some wood scraps. When dry, this will give you something to play around with to get your glaze to the right shade. You can also control it to some extent by the amount of wiping you do. The practice session helps even if you get a prepared glaze, letting you develop just the right touch in the wiping process.

The base coat is put on like any other paint job. Make sure the base coat is 100 percent dry before going on to the glazing. Don't take the attitude that the glaze will hide a bad paint job. It may hide some of your boo-boos, but it may not. Do it right! If it needs a second coat, give it one.

Now brush on the glaze. Take no pains with the application other than to make sure you get complete coverage of the part you're working on. Don't try to glaze too big a part at one time. While you have to wait until the glaze starts to dull before wiping it, if it gets too hard, you'll get a harsh look. The practice session on the scraps lets you know just about how much to rub off to achieve the effect you want. Where you want highlights, like in the center of a flat area, wipe away the glaze. In the corners, at the edges, or down in the indentations, leave it in. Then, in between, try to blend it.

The end result of the glaze is also governed by what you use to wipe with. The kits usually have a piece of cheesecloth. Almost anything you can grab will partially remove the glaze. I've known people to use such things as crumpled-up newspaper, steel wool, plastic wrap, aluminum foil, burlap, carpet scraps, nylon net, excelsior, or even an old pair of jockey shorts. Generally, the softer materials will remove more glaze, and thus leave an overall light haze. A coarser material will leave streaks. The idea is to experiment to find out just what the wiping material will do.

Speaking of streaks, graining is produced by pulling a dry brush across the already wiped—but not dry—glaze. It may take some practice to get it to look like wood grain. Some use a carpet scrap or steel wool instead of a brush. To me, the best-looking graining is the more subtle variety, but you may want it to jump out at you.

Another fun preglazing technique is spatterdashing or splattering. If you splatter in small dots, they can look like wormholes or flyspecks. Either effect is desirable. Larger blobs will just create an interesting effect. Here again, you've got to experiment to see what you can come up with.

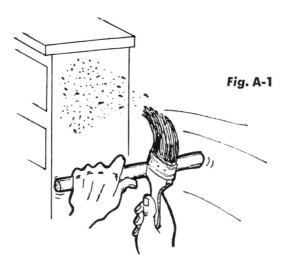

Fig. A-1

To get you started splattering, here are some basics. The most popular splatters are dark, almost black. However, if you want red ones, go to it. For the dark kind, use a thinned black or dark brown paint. Some folks mix color from a tube into turpentine, while others darken up the leftover base coat. Whatever you splatter with, make sure it's compatible with the base coat.

For the flyspeck/wormhole-size dots, you need a stiff-bristled brush like a toothbrush (make it an old one unless you want the splattered effect on your teeth.) Pour a little of the splatter glop in a mayonnaise jar lid and dip the bristles in. Hold the toothbrush a few inches from the work with the end aimed at the furniture. Now draw a stick—a Popsicle stick is great for this—across the bristles toward you, and you've just splattered. (Draw it the other way and you've just splattered your face.) A little practice will show you how much paint to load the brush with, how far away from the work it should be, and the best way to flick the stick in order to get the pattern you want.

Larger splatters are created by using a small- to medium-sized paint brush. Strike the loaded brush against a piece of broom handle or a stick, as shown in Fig. A-1. For a *really* authentic Early American spattered effect, you can try the corncob stippling that the Pennsylvania Dutch used on their furniture. For you city folk, you use corn on the cob *after* the kids are through with it. Let the cob dry for a week or two, until it's rough to the touch, then dip it lightly in a roller pan of whatever paint you want, and stipple away. Corncob stippling is entirely authentic, and though it can get quite messy, the effect is delightfully naïve and appealing, and if you wipe off any that spills on exposed moldings, you'll have an effect of wear that fools almost anyone into thinking you've got a real museum piece. Even when you 'fess up, they won't be able to figure out how the job was done.

Play around with splattering two or more contrasting colors. Use clear varnish, and while it's still wet, dust powder in gold or bronze over it. In short, create your own splatters.

After you've splattered, come in with the glaze, but make sure you test the glaze ahead of time to see that it won't dissolve or bleed the splatters. If it does, you will need to seal them before the glaze goes on.

Chapter **14**

Decals, Decoupage, and Gilding

There are all sorts of ways to decorate furniture after it's finished. Gilding and bronzing give a piece of furniture a regal look. Decoupage or the use of decals make for lively focal points on a furniture piece.

In addition to these conventional ways to decorate, I'll tell you about a few oddballs. However, the field is unlimited. Almost every month a magazine will come up with some unique and different new treatment for furniture. Chances are, if the decorating ideas here aren't far out enough, you could create some wild effect of your own.

DECALS

Decals are an excellent way to decorate inexpensive furniture in a kid's room. You can buy individual designs or sheets that have a motif. Decals are made for every age group. You can start out with bunny rabbits when he's an infant, and end up with college mascots or contemporary designs when adolescence rolls around.

When applying, make sure the finish underneath isn't going to dissolve with the water used for the decal. Also check to see if the color will fight the design on the decal.

Removing decals seems to be the biggest problem. Our kids always seemed to be able to do that for us. As infants they ate them, and as they grew older, they chopped them off along with chunks of the furniture. If yours have survived, here are a few tricks from the readers of my column:

A small sanding block (coarse grade) will take it off fast.

Make a compress of a couple of thicknesses of soft cloth. Saturate with either household ammonia or warm vinegar. As the decal softens, it can be wiped away.

Sponge with hot water. Press a blotter over the decal.

Or borrow the neighbor's kids.

DECOUPAGE

Decoupage is very big as a craft. It can also be used to decorate furniture. I'll not go into the various methods because your local hobby or craft store will teach you, sell you the materials, and have a selection of prints to apply. Besides, almost everyone is a decoupager already anyway.

I will issue this word of warning: Decoupage is habit-forming. No one seems to be able to decoupage in moderation. The person who really gets into it ends up with eighty-five decoupaged wall hangings plus four to eight decoupaged areas on every piece of furniture.

The best use of decoupage on furniture is to use it only to highlight one or two pieces in the entire house.

GILDING

Gilding is done either with powder or leaf. The use of powder in gilding is sometimes called bronzing. It is more popular with us amateur gilders because it's easier and faster. However, it doesn't do as good a job as leaf gilding because after a while, powder loses the shiny metallic look.

Whichever method you use will require a little practice before you become proficient. A picture frame is a good place to start.

For either powder or leaf, the first steps are the same. The wood need not be super smooth, but if just stripped or new, it should be sealed. The best surface on which to gild is one covered with gesso. Two or three coats with a light sanding and cleaning after each coat will give you the surface. Now apply two coats of a dull red artist's acrylic paint. Sand after each coat. This dull red adds a great deal to the richness of the gilt. A special sizing called gilder's burnish red-gold size is even better—if available—than the acrylic.

Powder — Now you're ready for the powder. When you go to buy it, you'll find there is also bronzing liquid, and that the powder can be mixed to form a liquid that is easily brushed on. Gold paint can also be easily brushed on, and the results of painting or gilding are about the same. If that's all you want, buy gold paint and skip this part. Getting good gilding is a time-consuming job.

The process involves putting on the piece a glue coat called "final size." When this gets tacky, the powder is dusted on. The art store will probably have only one kind of final size. It'll be either a varnish base or lacquer base. The instructions will be on the container, but you should know that varnish base takes from ten to twenty-four hours to get tacky, while lacquer base comes around in a half hour or so. If you have a choice, the time element can be the deciding factor.

When the surface is tacky, it will feel sticky, but won't actually stick to your finger.

When it's tacky, you should start powdering. The best method is to take a small scrap of velvet and dip it gently into the powder. Very lightly rub the powder onto the tacky surface. You'll find that just that one gentle dip will go a long way.

When the desired overall appearance is reached, let the thing sit for a full twenty-four hours. Remove any loose powder with a vacuum cleaner, but don't actually touch the surface with the vacuum.

A protective finish of clear shellac, lacquer, or varnish is a good idea because a powdered-gilt surface is fragile. This dulls the gold shine ever so slightly, but it's a must unless it's on something that gets no wear.

Gold Leaf — Using gold leaf is called "gilding in the wind." That's sort of a romantic expression, and I have no idea where it came from or why it's not called "gilding up a rope" or "gilding in your ear." Whatever you call it, it's a difficult task.

It starts being difficult when you find that the sheets of gold leaf you bought have wrinkles in them. You then quickly find the sheets are larger than you can handle and have to be cut. But the surface side is so extremely delicate that it can't be touched with the fingers!

The wrinkles can be taken out by burnishing. Then you must practice to get to the point where you can apply this thin leaf without wrinkling it as it's placed down, and without touching the top side.

Cutting is done with very sharp scissors, and the leaf must be held between the two sheets of tissue paper backing that came with it.

The tackiness test applies here too. As for handling, pick up the leaf with the tissue on the side facing out. Then gently lay it in place. Use a cotton ball to smooth it with the tissue still in place. You start laying the leaf at one edge and work in a pattern as shown by the numbered squares in Fig. G-1. Each piece of leaf will overlap the adjoining leaf by about ⅛-inch. You will always rub in one direction so as to go back over the overlap instead of against it, as shown in Fig. G-2. If, after the tissue is removed, you see wrinkles or bubbles, use a soft brush to smooth them out. Here again, brush over the overlaps.

After the final size is completely dry (the label will tell you how long), gently rub off any loose overlaps. Burnishing is done with a stone you can get from the art store where you bought the leaf. It's usually agate, but sometimes is flint. A certain amount of burnishing can be done with a soft flannel-like rag.

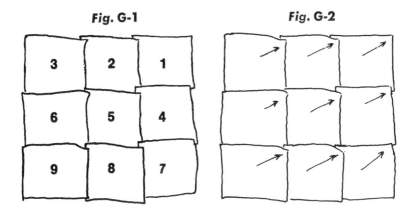

Fig. G-1   **Fig. G-2**

There are lots of other ways to do almost every step of gilding. They work too. What I've passed on here are the simplest I've come across. If the expert at the art store uses another method, he's probably right too.

Now that you know the basics, there are lots of ways to use gilding. Highlighting carved pieces with gold is good. Antiquing over the gold with a glaze grabs some folks. Painting over the entire piece of furniture and then rubbing off over the gilded areas gives a nice effect. You can come up with all sorts of combinations.

Gilded stenciling can produce striking results. After the final size is down, press the cutout in place on the tacky surface. Then apply the powder as described previously. A light coat is called for, and care should be used not to get the bronzing dust under the stencil.

Maybe you'll want to try a combination of bronzing and painting. If so, do the gilding last and give it a protective coating as with regular powder gilding.

Striping is also done in combination with gilding the powder way. You just substitute the final size for the paint.

Part Three

MAINTENANCE AND CREATION

There is a lot more to the furniture game than fixing a broken leg or slapping a coat of something on to make the piece look pretty. If you can learn a few good tricks on taking care of your furniture, you'll avoid some messy jobs. Also, all of the problems solved in this book so far have dealt with woods and their finishes. But a lot of furniture isn't all wood and certainly you should be able to take care of this furniture as well. And just in case you don't have enough furniture to fret over, there are even some ways to create some things on your own.

Chapter **15**

Protecting Your Furniture

No matter how much you enjoy fixing and finishing, it's not a job you want to tackle every six months—not on the same piece of furniture, anyway.

A lot of the work that has to be done in fixing and finishing furniture could be avoided with the right kind of protection. Naturally you can't leave your living room furniture out on the patio and expect it to last too long. The easy solution is, of course, to leave it inside the house. Well, even in the house, extra steps need to be taken to preserve your furniture.

A nice sunny atmosphere in a home is great. However, the sun coming through the windows can fade both the upholstery and the finish on furniture. Keep this in mind in the arrangement, and if you have to end up with a couch right in the window, keep the drapes drawn during the time when direct sunlight hits that window.

Some areas have very humid climates. This extra humidity gets into the house and into your furniture. Exposed wood drinks in this moisture and swells, causing stuck drawers. Mildew can form on furniture.

While too much moisture ruins furniture, too little can also do damage. In the winter, many heating systems provide air of very low relative humidity, which causes woods to shrink and crack. Joints are pulled loose by the shrinkage.

What you should do about correcting the humidity within your house depends largely on the type of heating system you have. A dehumidifier in summer is easy, but having the correct moisture situation in winter will also make your home more comfortable and will increase the efficiency of the heating and air-conditioning systems. So figure it out and seek guidance from the heating and air-conditioning folks.

Dirt is also a furniture fouler. So clean the house every month or so. . . even if it doesn't need it. Clean air is better on furniture, and so change or clean filters regularly.

FANCY FOOTWORK—GLIDES, CASTERS, AND RESTS

A beautifully finished chair that rocks when it's not a rocking chair isn't so beautiful to live with. Nor is a bed that has to be pulled out each day to be made up, but has no rollers. Also, when you move a heavy piece and find it's dug a hole in the floor, you can't be too happy about it.

All of these problems and a lot more are solved by using the right kind of footwork on the legs of furniture.

Adjustable casters and glides can compensate for either an uneven piece of furniture or an uneven floor. Having them in place means you can compensate for changes that occur without sticking a matchbook under one leg.

There are eighty zillion different kinds. To get the right kind, be sure to get one that's right for the floor it'll be on. Where casters are concerned, be sure to get those capable of carrying the weight of the furniture piece. If the piece is a sofa, chair, or bed, consider the weight of the furniture plus its occupants.

When you need to replace casters, it's a good idea to make the replacements a better quality than the original equipment. Many manufacturers don't go all out on casters.

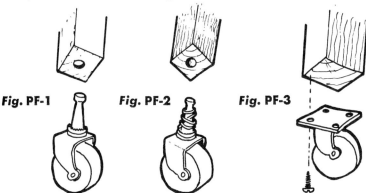

Fig. PF-1   Fig. PF-2   Fig. PF-3

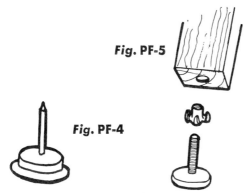

Fig. PF-5

Fig. PF-4

Basically, casters are attached to furniture in one of three ways. A stem caster (Fig. PF-1) uses a socket adapter that slips into a hole in the bottom of the leg. Then the stem on the caster snaps right into the socket. If this type of caster gets loose, wire or a rubber band wound around the stem will help (Fig. PF-2). Plate casters (Fig. PF-3) are flat on top, and screws are used to attach them to the leg. Spring adapters are for use in tubular metal legs.

Glides are often made with a sharp point which is hammered into the bottom of the leg (Fig. PF-4). Some have three points, and others only one. Pilot holes are a good idea before whocking them into the furniture. Others are installed just as the stem casters are. Others are threaded to fit in a threaded socket called a tee nut (Fig. PF-5). One type of glide has a tilting stem that adjusts for use with angled legs.

Rests are generally little rubber or plastic cups placed under furniture legs to protect the floor. Watch out for the glass kind, however—they can break unexpectedly when too much weight is applied.

Sectional pieces of furniture are apparently made to repel one another. They always seem to be separating, and the parts crawl in opposite directions. Screen door hooks and eyes can be installed at the right places so the parts can be joined together, but can easily be unhitched when they need to be. This same idea is good for a couch that keeps walking away from its station against the wall.

If you have kids in your home, you must take a different tack with your furniture. Unfortunately, the cartoons that show kids in the act of furniture demolition are all true. This means that not only do you have to worry about the fixing and finishing of furniture . . . there's a third *F*: fortifying.

Throughout the house, you should make sure all your best furniture is out of the general lanes of youngster traffic . . . like against a wall. Then arrange other pieces to go in front as a sort of blockade.

With kids around, regular waxing is a must. The wax is a semiprotection against fingerprints, tricycle handlebars, and all sorts of other things. The legs of chairs and tables often get bumped or gouged by passing toys. One way to avoid constant refinishing is to get yourself a "sleeve" of black foam rubber that can be attached to the leg with rubber bands. If you make a matching sleeve for the other three legs, the final effect will not look all that bad; but in any case, these shoulder pads slip off easily when company comes or your children grow up—whichever comes first.

While the furniture throughout the house takes a beating, the stuff within a child's room is brutally assaulted daily. Consequently, you may be in for more regular work. Here are a few things to keep in mind.

In an infant's room, *be sure* to use a nontoxic, lead-free paint. This should be an unnecessary thought to toss in, but every year some of our smaller citizens get lead poisoning. I suspect it's because "there was this leftover paint, and it looked fine in the kid's room." Also, in the preparation, make sure you leave no sharp edges, rough spots, splinters, or exposed nails.

If you're going to buy furniture, you don't have to go in for special nursery stuff except for the bed. Regular chests and dressers can be made to look right in the nursery with the right paint and/or decorations. If you go this route, look for pieces tall enough so the adults can take care of the baby with a minimum of bending over.

For a child's room, whether infant or teenager, you might consider the tops of tables, dressers, and the like as good candidates for Plexiglas tops. This will save lots of spots from spills, soft drinks, craft projects, or nail polish.

Handprints getting you down? A coat of spray starch over painted furniture in a child's room will aid in the clean-up and the protection of the finish. When the dirt gets too bad, take a

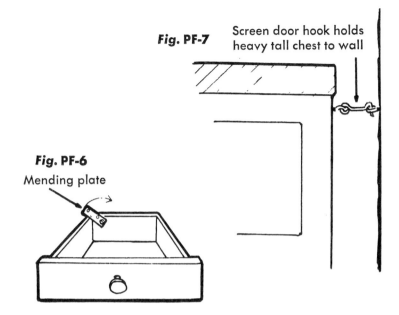

Fig. PF-7

Screen door hook holds
heavy tall chest to wall

Fig. PF-6

Mending plate

damp cloth and remove the dirt and starch. None of the dirt will have penetrated the starch, so the wood will be unharmed. Of course, a new coat of starch is then called for.

When kids pass infancy, they move their furniture around, and so I suggest you make sure all legs have glides of some sort. Also, it's not a bad idea to put bumpers on pieces that seem to be constantly getting banged in the same places. Another thing that children do is to pull drawers out too far. This is not only dangerous to the child and the floor, but can also damage the furniture. Install stops in the backs of all drawers. The one in Fig. PF-6 is just a metal mending plate. The screw holding it is loose enough so the stop can be rotated down out of the way when *you* want to take the drawer completely out.

Another danger is with tall pieces. Kids sometimes climb on them. A screen door hook anchoring the back to the wall (Fig. PF-7) will keep the furniture from tipping over so easily.

We've already suggested the protection of wax for furniture throughout the house. Most people forget that wastebaskets are also furniture. A wax job *inside* the wastebasket in a child's room will keep all sorts of things from sticking to the bottom . . . bubble gum included.

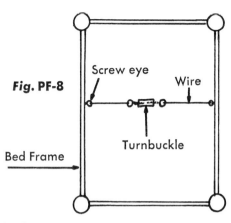

Fig. PF-8

Screw eye

Wire

Turnbuckle

Bed Frame

With kids around, the bed just has to double as a part-time trampoline. This creates a bed slat dropout problem which can lead to the total collapse of the bed. Here are a few of the ways my readers have come up with to fight this. Install two screw eyes in the side frame so you can run a wire across the middle of the bed. Place a turnbuckle in the center of the wire as shown in Fig. PF-8. When all the slats are in place, turn the turnbuckle as tight as possible, and this pulls the side rails very tight against the slat ends. Even an Olympic tumbler will have trouble getting the slats to fall out.

Another approach is to drill holes through the slat ends and on through the frame. Drop large nails (Fig. PF-9) in the holes, and they will anchor the slats until you want to lift the nails out. (If you spend much time hiding under the bed, snip the points off the nails first.)

If you don't have a big problem with slat dropout, slip wide rubber bands around the ends of the slats to make them skid-proof.

One reader attached hinges to the slats as shown in Fig. PF-10. He used the kind with removable hinge pins. The other leaf was attached to the frame. Then with the pin in place, the slat was firmly attached to the bed. By the time you do this to both ends of all the slats, you have invested a bit of work.

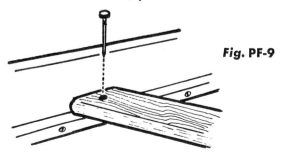

Fig. PF-9

The problem of separate rooms for two kids was solved nicely by one father. He got bunk beds for his boys, then closed off opposite sides of each bunk with a piece of wall paneling cut to fit. The beds were placed in the center of the room and acted as a divider, and since each boy climbed out of bed on opposite sides, it was as if they were each in their own room. He added a folding door, attached to the end of the bunks, to complete the separation.

If the kids are teenagers, you'll find that their tastes can change regularly . . . sometimes only weeks after you've refinished the furniture in their room. It behooves you to use the simplest forms of finish—paints—for teen quarters. That way, when one fad expires, it's not as big a chore to redo. What really solves this problem, however, is to get the teenager involved in the refinishing. They can actually do the whole thing and should. (You can supervise.) This may make them think twice before changing the decor. (If you find out how to get your teenagers to do this, write a book on the subject and make a fortune.)

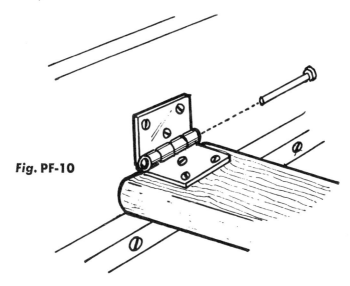

Fig. PF-10

Chapter **16**

First Aid for Fabrics

Upholstered furniture can mean anything from a dining chair with a covered seat up to a couch. It's a field all its own, and there's not enough space in this book to cover it completely. However, I think it well to know a few basics. Then if you decide to progress in the upholstery game, you can seek more detailed information.

Upholstered furniture can often be cleaned rather than re-covered. However, I have to admit that I fall apart here. The few times I've tried to remove spots it hasn't worked out too well. I'd be afraid to try to shampoo an entire upholstered piece. However, both spot removal and upholstery shampooing are do-it-yourself projects and can be done successfully.

While not doing too well at spot removal, I have learned a few things. Combine that with advice from my wife and a few pros, and maybe these pointers will help:

1. Always vacuum clean the entire area before any effort is made to remove a stain.
2. If the overall piece is soiled, don't try to lift a specific spot. You'll be trading a spot of grease for a spot of clean. The clean ring may show up more than the old spot.

3. Test the spot remover on an obscure part of the fabric, if possible, to find out if it does weird things to it.
4. Get on stains as soon as possible.
5. If there's any doubt about what the spot is or any doubt about what that particular cleaner will do to the fabric, take it to a pro. If it's a valuable treasure, I'd certainly be sure before I'd tackle it—and, in my case, even though I've seen it work, I've never been that sure. When in doubt, you'll do better to let a professional do this job.

Now, here is a list of things that leave stains on upholstery, what can be used to remove them, and how to use it:

UPHOLSTERY STAIN REMOVAL CHART

(Super Handyman's Nonguaranteed but Sometimes Lucky Methods)

STAIN	WHAT TO DO
Acids	Neutralize pronto. Baking soda in water, white vinegar, or ammonia will neutralize . . . but test first for color-fastness.
Booze and other alcoholic spills	Sponge with cloth barely damp with denatured alcohol. In its absence, use water.
Blood	If you get on it before it dries, cold water or cold salt water will probably do it. If old stain, mix a few drops of ammonia in one half cup of water. If spot is still there, try to sponge off with hydrogen peroxide.
Candle wax	Try to chip away with a dull knife. Sometimes holding an ice cube against the wax makes it more brittle. If candle dye leaves a stain, use a cleaning fluid and follow directions.
Chewing gum	Try to chip or scrape away. An ice cube held against it will make it more brittle. If any is still left, cleaning fluid will usually complete the job. Some swear by egg white as a gum softener. It is then picked away.
Chocolate	Scrape off excess. Sponge in cool water. When dry, use cleaning fluid.
Coffee	Blot, sponge with water. If it was black coffee, that's probably all you'll need to do. If it had cream, a cleaning fluid should be used after the sponged area is dry.

Grease	Most folks try an adsorbent first. Make a paste of cornstarch and cover the spot. When dry, brush it off. You may have to do this a couple of times. Usually you have to finish with cleaning fluid . . . so that's what I start with. Some people combine the two steps by using the cleaning fluid to make the paste.
Hair oil	If the wet head isn't dead around your house, cleaning fluid will at least kill his tracks.
Ink	This is a toughy because there are several types of inks. Try an adsorbent made with cream of tartar. Apply and when dry, brush away. Several tries with cleaning fluid usually are the best go. India ink can sometimes be removed with a mild ammonia and water sponging . . . which can sometimes also remove the color in your fabric.
Mud	Let it dry. Then take a stiff brush and brush it away.
Paint	Check the label to see what solvent is required. Then if the solvent won't affect your fabric, and if the paint is still wet, you can often remove the spot. After it's dry, you can try all the cleaning fluids. Maybe you'll find one that works.
Soft drinks	Blot the spill immediately, and then sponge with cool water. Repeat.
Wine	Blot it up quickly. Sponge with cool salt water. Sponge with plain water. Apply an adsorbent paste of cornstarch and water. When dry, brush away. Repeat.

Warning: Always test on an obscure part of the upholstery before you try anything on it.

Now for the shampoo bit. There are electrically operated upholstery shampooers that can be rented at some hardware stores. There are aerosol shampoos on the market, and there are manually operated units. All operate by putting foam on the upholstery and then removing the dirty lather before it soaks in. The key is to never let the foam stay on long enough to get the fabric really wet. Also, using an electric fan afterwards will remove the dampness quicker, and thus preclude it going through. All three of the above methods come with instructions. *Follow* them!

Stale beer is a good solution to use to clean leather furniture. When you have gone over the surface, wipe it off with a damp cloth. (I've never let beer get stale . . . had to borrow some to try this.)

Chapter **17**

Reupholstery

When recovering kitchen chairs with vinyl that has to be stretched over the edges before stapling, you'll find the stuff forms easier if it's heated a little. One reader suggested a hot water bottle, while another solved the problem with a warm iron over a cup towel.

FABRIC COVERING

Another decorative way to finish is to cover all or part of wooden pieces with fabric. If there's much to be covered, it's best to make a paper pattern. After the fabric is cut, spread a thin layer of white all-purpose glue on the section to be covered. Smooth the fabric out and overlap any corners. If the edges of cloth can be brought underneath, staple them in place. It's best to test a swatch of the fabric before you start to be sure the glue doesn't do wicked things to the dyes.

To apply needlepoint to existing upholstery, cut away the excess canvas, tuck the seam allowance under the needlepoint and steam press it to get it to lie as flat as possible. Then baste it to the back. Whipstitch it in place on the upholstery. Hide the stitches with gimp or braid.

There are lots of other kinky things you can do to decorate furniture pieces. As you go creative and come up with some weirdos, let me know what happens. But most upholstered pieces start with a wooden frame. The same principles of frame repair apply to upholstered furniture, except for the fact that here the frame will be covered. That means you can do a fairly sloppy job and then hide it under padding and fabric. However, don't be so slipshod that the frame isn't sturdy. It's disconcerting when you finish a beautifully upholstered couch that collapses. Since it will all be hidden, extra sturdiness can be built in with added glue blocks, metal mending plates and whatever else. In repairing a frame that will be covered, you don't have to match wood in replacing broken parts, or be careful with your hammering.

However, there are other things involved in such a piece. Usually there will be springs. If they are coil springs, they are probably held at the proper level by strong cord, and normally will rest on webbing attached to the frame.

On top, around the sides, and often at the back there will be padding of some sort covered with fabric.

Since you already know how to deal with wooden frame repairs, let's see what can be done about webbing. Many times the webbing can be attacked from underneath without removing the upholstery fabric. Flip the piece over. There should be a piece of lightweight cloth called cambric tacked or stapled to the bottom. Remove this, and you'll see the webbing. If webbing is tacked to the bottom of the frame, you can repair or replace it without having to dismantle the upholstery on top.

Generally, upholstered furniture has springs within the basic wooden frame. There are three basic types of springing systems: (1) the coil spring (Fig. U-1), (2) the zigzag (Fig. U-2), and (3) the strap and coil springs (Fig. U-3).

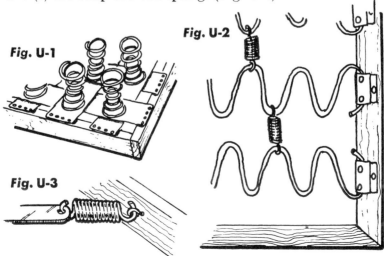

Fig. U-1

Fig. U-2

Fig. U-3

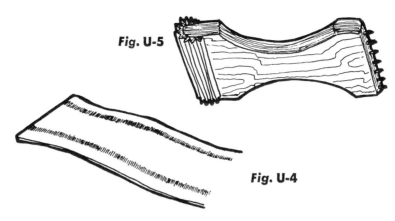

Fig. U-5

Fig. U-4

The coil springs are most often used in furniture and are available in many diameters, heights, and gauges. These coils are generally tied together with twine to hold them at the desired height.

The springs are supported by webbing. Mostly this is webbing like I've illustrated in Fig. U-4. The springs will be sewn to the webbing to keep them in place. However, the "webbing" may turn out to be heavy wirelike supports attached to the frame. In some cases, the "webbing" is just a plywood base.

Beneath the webbing (even if it ain't webbed) there's usually a dust cover. I suspect this is a misnomer because there seems to be more trouble with stuffing coming out than with dust going in.

Above the springs, there's usually a layer of burlap, and over it the stuffing, covered by the fabric you see. In between any of these different layers, you may find other layers of material. The material may be lightweight, almost like cheesecloth, or heavy like burlap.

If you've got a sagging couch, you may be able to get inside and retie the spring that's gone *boing* . . . or it may be only the webbing that has stretched out of shape.

First, remove the dust cover. If the webbing is sagging, it will have to be restretched. In order to do this, you'll need a tool called webbing pliers. They have wide-grooved jaws that allow you to grip and stretch the webbing. If the webbing is damaged, you'll want to replace it, which is easy to do. The tool in Fig. U-5 is an inexpensive stretcher, called a strainer in some circles.

However, if the webbing has begun to give way, even in only one or two places, it's best to replace the entire web job. If you don't, chances are the strips you didn't replace will give way next week. After all, they're the same age as the ones that have to be replaced. Also, the new strips will be more resistant which could make the seat sit cattywampus.

In replacing all the webbing, not only do you mark on the frame where the strips go, but it's also smart to make a sketch showing the spring arrangement. Getting them spaced back in properly will restore the chair to its proper shape.

While you've got the chair innards uncovered, check to be sure all the springs are still properly tied. See if any of the padding has been displaced. If there are layers of cloth (usually burlap) between springs and padding, be sure it's not torn. Wandering padding can usually be pushed back in place from underneath, and any torn fabric can be patched. You'll never have a better opportunity to vacuum the darn thing, and a clean chair is a happy chair . . . for those with allergies.

It's also a good idea to fill in the old tack holes with wood dough. Since you have to wait for it to set up, it's a legitimate excuse to procrastinate.

Okay, back to work. You're going to put all the strips running in one direction in place before weaving the crosspieces. Line up the end of the webbing with a mark on the frame, leaving about one and a half inches hanging over the edge. Drive in two tacks as shown in Fig. U-6. Now take the one and a half inch hangover and make a fold as in Fig. U-7. Next tack the fold down. Stagger the line of tacks. It'll give greater strength, and there'll be less likelihood of splitting the wood if you don't set the tacks in a straight line. The outside tacks should be about a half inch in from the edge to leave tacking room for the dust

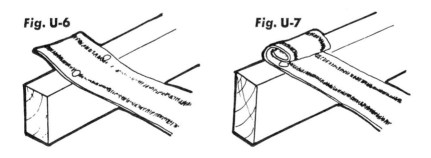

Fig. U-6   **Fig. U-7**

cover. In some cases, the outside fabric will already be tacked under the frame, so you'll have to avoid it. Your tacked, folded web should look like the one in Fig. U-8 . . . or better.

Now you're ready for the strainer or stretcher. The idea is to insert the spikes in the web at a point that will allow the padded end to rest against the outside of the frame at about the angle shown in Fig. U-9. This will take a little fiddling around to get it just right. Then the stretcher is pressed down, and the webbing is pulled really tight across the frame. There are four cautions: (1) Don't get it so tight it mangles the frame, (2) Don't get it so tight it breaks the webbing, (3) Don't pull the tacks out at the other end, and (4) Don't stab yourself on the spikes.

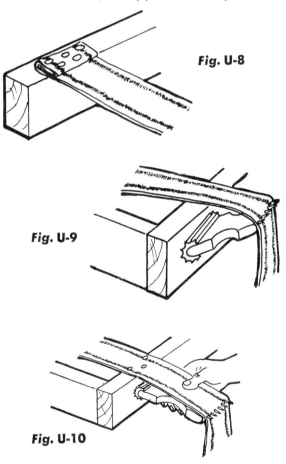

Fig. U-8

Fig. U-9

Fig. U-10

Once it's tight as a drum (it *should* make a drumlike sound when whocked), tack it down while still holding your stretcher in place. This time use three tacks as shown in Fig. U-10. Now you can let go and reach for the Band-Aids.

Next, cut off the webbing, leaving about one and a half inches for another fold. Tack the fold in place, and you're ready for the next strip.

When the strips are in all the way across, start on the cross strips. They go on the same way except each strip is interwoven after one end is tacked in place.

As you web, the springs will get in the way, so you'll need to push them over so they don't prevent the proper tension on the webbing. With the webbing all in place, though, you must carefully relocate all the spring bottoms to their proper place on the webbing. When all springs are back in place, flip the chair upright to see that it looks right, and then sew the springs to the webbing. Each spring is attached in four places. Replace the dust cover, and the job is done.

We mentioned that the springs should be checked to be sure they are still tied at the top. Usually you can retie by looking at the ones still intact. Fig. U-11 shows a typical pattern of stringing, and Fig. U-12 shows a close-up of how each spring is tied. There may be more or less springs, and this would change the stringing pattern, but you get the idea.

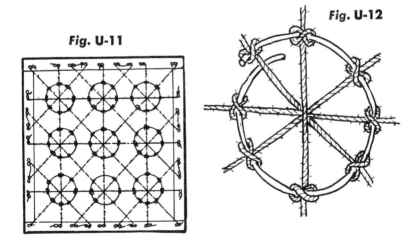

Fig. U-12

Fig. U-11

Fig. U-13

Two-tack tie

Fig. U-14

One-tack tie

The strings are attached to the frame by looping them around tacks. Figs. U-13 and U-14 show the two most popular ways. The problem you encounter in just repairing is that these tacks have been driven down after the knot was made. If you can get at the tacks in the frame, they can be pried out and replaced when the string is retied. If not, you may have to sew the springs that are loose to the burlap above. Or maybe you do something unorthodox and tie to tacks on the side of the frame. With luck, the break in the string will not be at the frame, and you can splice new twine in. Probably the only way to do it according to the rules is to remove the padding and cover, but we're looking for easier ways.

If you want to recover the entire piece, you'll have to take the covering off. Take it off carefully. The pieces of the old cover will be the pattern for the new cover. Also note how the covering was tacked into place and how the pieces were sewn together. The new covering doesn't have to go back the same way, but you'll need a more complete upholstery cover to do it differently. While it's off, inspect the padding and any other layers of fabric.

If the padding has lost its pizzazz, replace it. Remember the padding not only makes the furniture safer, it also gives it shape. If it's on a part of furniture where people sit, it must be resilient enough to spring back up when 230-pound Aunt Minnie gets up.

Maybe the old fiber stuffing can be revived. What the heck, it's worth a try. For the home stuffing reviver, it's a matter of handpicking little bits of the fibers to break up the packed-down parts. As you pick and pull, overlap with fibers underneath to keep it all as one unit.

In many cases, there'll be more than one layer of stuffing. Ideally there are three. The bottom layer is probably coarse and semi-resilient. The second stuffing will be very resilient, and the top padding will be soft and smooth. Pick each layer separately. They may be separated by cloth, but if not don't blend them together with your fluffing.

If the stuffing must be replaced, you'd best seek advice from your upholstery supplier. He'll be able to tell you what type you need to do the right job, and let you know ahead of time what you're getting into. He may not suggest the same type of stuffing you're taking out.

Foam rubber stuffings are quite popular. They may be used in conjunction with fiber stuffings or you may use only the foam. It comes in different densities, and you can have three layers of foam of different densities.

Cutting foam is best done when the material is fully compressed. Place a wide board next to the line to be cut, and then push down. As good a cutting tool as you'll find is an electric carving knife. One of the readers of my column sent that in as a hint, and I thought she was pulling my leg. Try it. It works pretty well. (I don't know what it does for the knife . . . we haven't had turkey since then.)

Another way to cut foam rubber padding is with a paper cutter. Those big cutter blades will give compressed padding a smooth, straight cut.

Now, if you tackle a re-covering job, don't start with a piece that has buttons, tufting, channels, or other fancy stuff. When you take the old covering apart to use as a pattern, take note of how the seams were made. Leave a little more seam allowance than is on the old fabric. You can trim off later if need be.

When the new cover is all together or the parts that go together are sewn, you'll want to start tacking. I suggest you take some warm-up strokes with your tack hammer. If the tacks will show, they must be perfectly lined up and spaced to look

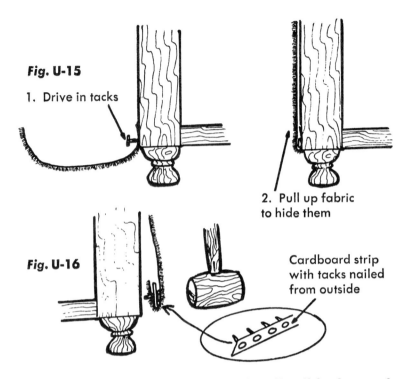

Fig. U-15

1. Drive in tacks

2. Pull up fabric to hide them

Fig. U-16

Cardboard strip with tacks nailed from outside

good. If they are underneath, the job will still be better if properly tacked.

Blind tacking is where the tacks are made on the back side of the fabric, and it's then folded back over the tacks (Fig. U-15). That's fine for all but the last side. For this, you cut a strip of cardboard to conform to the edge. Position tacks in the strip with your thumb. Pull the fabric around this as shown in Fig. U-16. Now you can tap in the tacks from the outside. However, be sure to tap with a well-padded hammer.

If the piece has end panels on the arms, they are easy to replace. After the padded panel is covered, it is then attached in place either by gluing or nailing. If glue is used, hot melt is good because it sets up fast. Just run the glue gun over the back of the panel in enough places to hold, and then press it into place. You should keep pressing for several minutes to be sure the glue has hardened. Nailing is done by driving the nails through the panel before covering it. Then a padded hammer and a layer of towels can drive the nail points into the frame.

If you really want to get into the upholstery bag, there are books and schools that can make you an expert. What we've tried to do is give you enough on the subject so you can try it and decide if it grabs you. One thing for sure, this can save you a ton of money over having it done.

Chapter 18

Caning Chair Bottoms

Possibly the biggest bargain to be had in buying used furniture is in chairs that have lost their bottoms. Until someone re-weaves with new cane, splint, raffia, rush, reed, or whatever, the chair is truly worthless. To have this done could run $50, and when the chair only cost that much twenty years ago, the owner is silently snickering as he unloads it on you for a buck or two.

Now you're not going to spend $50 to restore it. You're going to invest time and a few dollars for a caning kit. Almost every magazine in the do-it-yourself field, and all the so-called shelter magazines, will have an ad or two on caning kits. Get their catalog and get the right size, type, and style kit. Not only will you get all the materials to do the job, but all kits also come with easy-to-follow, beautifully detailed instructions. Some even have tools. I defy almost anyone to buy a kit for chair bottoms and not come up with at least a decent job.

After you've conquered a kit or two, you can then buy the materials separately and save even more. Kits start at a few dollars, and on these less expensive bottoms, the materials bought separately would cost about half as much.

WEAVING CANE

To give you a clue as to how really easy caning can be, let's recane a small area. First, remove all the old stuff. You can usually cut it away with large shears. Make sure the holes are cleaned out—an ice pick will do this. It's also a good idea to sand the frame edges if they're sharp. Naturally, any refinishing must be done now . . . before caning begins.

You can tell what size cane to order by checking the hole sizes and by measuring the distance between the holes. The Cane Chart tells you what size cane to order, and also gives you the names of the various types.

CANE CHART

Cane Type	Distance Between Holes	Hole Diameter
Carriage	$3/8''$	$1/8''$
Super fine	$3/8''$	$1/8''$
Fine fine	$1/2''$	$3/16''$
Fine	$5/8''$	$3/16''$
Medium	$3/4''$	$1/4''$
Common	$7/8''$	$5/16''$

Any one kit will have enough for a chair. If you're going to order the cane in bulk, however, you usually have to buy a bundle, which is enough for three chairs. Some places will sell by the half bundle. The longer the strands, the less tying you have to do, so if there's a choice, go for long.

To make the cane workable, let it soak in a bowl of warm water. When it becomes pliable, you can start working with it. As you work, occasionally dunk your hands in the water, and as you pull on the cane, this will keep it pliable. Some cane people put a little glycerine in the soaking water and claim this keeps the cane damp, so it stays soft and pliable longer.

Don't put the next strand in the water until you're just about ready for it, since oversoaking leaves it too soggy to work with. Different sizes require different amounts of time in the bowl to get to just the right stage.

The seat we're doing is wider at the front than back as shown

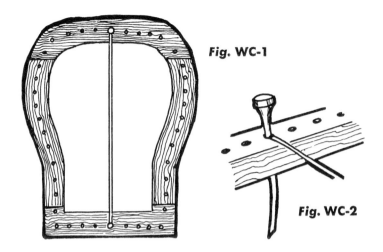

Fig. WC-1

Fig. WC-2

in the frame in Fig. WC-1. We start the weaving at the middle and put a peg in the middle holes at both the front and back. (Golf tees make good caning pegs.) Lift up the back peg and insert the cane in the hole, then fasten it in place with the peg (Fig. WC-2). Leave four to six inches hanging out. Now run the cane down to the front middle hole, remove the peg, run the cane through, pull it almost tight, and reinsert the peg. Now you're going to work toward the side by bringing the cane up through the next hole and running it parallel to the first strand. Since the back is narrower than the front, in order to keep the strands parallel, we use appropriate side holes as shown in Fig. WC-3.

As you go along, keep the smooth, shiny side of the cane facing up, and don't twist it. Make sure all strands have the same degree of almost-tightness.

When you get to the end of a strand, put it through the last hole that will allow at least four inches hanging under, and peg it.

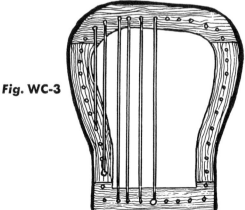

Fig. WC-3

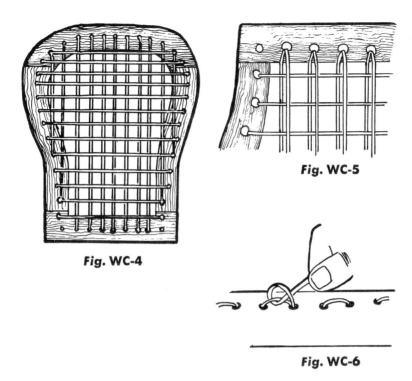

Fig. WC-5

Fig. WC-4

Fig. WC-6

After you've done the other half from front to back, you're ready to start doing the same thing from side to side. For this, we start at the back hole, doing the same sort of thing, and work all the way up to the front. It should now look sort of like Fig. WC-4.

Now you're ready to put another series of back-to-front strands in over what you've done. You use the same holes and same methods. However, keep all these top strands slightly to the right of the first strands (Fig. WC-5).

When this step is all done, you need to tie off the ends underneath. Otherwise you'll end up with eighty-seven pegs, and at least half will be in the way. The tying is done by knotting the end around the little crossover strand made underneath as you changed from one row to another. Fig. WC-6 shows how this is done. If these tails have dried out and become stiff, dampen them so you can tie without breaking them off. Those at the starting points won't have a crossover strand yet, so just keep them pegged. Snip off the tails of the strands you've tied.

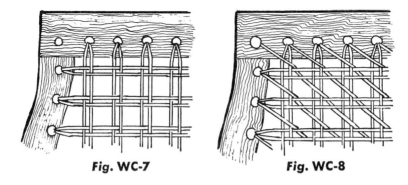

Fig. WC-7   **Fig. WC-8**

We used the word "weaving" before, but until now there hasn't been any. But on the next side-to-side series, we'll actually be working the cane strand over and under the back-to-front jobs as shown in Fig. WC-7. You start back at the last hole on the right, and work forward on the first cross strands, going over, then under. About halfway, pull the strand all the way through. If it's hard to pull through, do it more often. Be careful to keep the strand untwisted and the front side up. As you go along, keep the strands snugged up in pairs. At the end of each row, when you put the cane down in the hole, peg it until you start weaving back the other way and pulling the strand through. When weaving back, left to right, your procedure is under first and then over.

When you've finished all the way on the side-to-side holes, tie down the tails again. An overall straightening is due now. Snug up at each corner to form uniform hollow squares. Pegs are better than fingers for this.

Now you're ready for the diagonal weaving. This starts in the heretofore unused hole in the back righthand corner. Peg the cane strand. Come over the back-to-front pair and then under the side-to-side pair as in Fig. WC-8. You may have to dampen the part already done, as well as keeping the strand you're working with wet. When you get to the hole diagonally across (it won't be the front corner unless the seat is square), go under to the next hole along the side. Bring the cane back through, and make sure it goes under the side-to-side and over the back-to-front pairs. When you've done this all the way back to the corner, peg or tie it and do the same sort of thing to the other half.

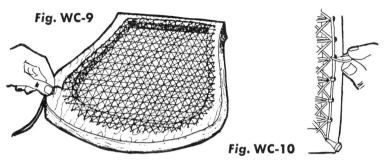

Fig. WC-9

Fig. WC-10

With all the strands running diagonally that way, you're ready to do the same thing diagonally the other way . . . only opposite. Start at the left rear corner and run *under* the back-to-front and *over* the side-to-side pairs. The weave should look like Fig. WC-9.

To finish the job, you need a piece of wider cane. In a kit, they supply this. If you don't have a kit, use two or three strands of the cane you've been weaving with. This is called the finishing binder. Cut a binder long enough to go all the way around the line of holes, with about eight inches left over. Peg the binder in one back corner and carefully lay it in place. Tie a long strand of the regular cane underneath and next to the corner. Bring this up through the first hole, over the binder, and back through the same hole as shown in Fig. WC-10. Pull it tight and proceed, doing the same thing at each hole all the way around. When you reach the starting point, remove the peg and turn the corner with the binder. Run the end of the binder down the first hole around the corner, and tie it. Tie off the strand you've been securing the binder with, as well as anything else that hasn't been tied. The job is done except for snipping off the tails and any hairs that may be sticking up.

Toward the end, there are quite a few strands already in some holes. You may need to use a nail or an awl to help get the darn stuff through. There are several other methods of caning, but the basic steps and weaving are just about the same.

Cane looks pretty good as is, but some folks put a coat of lacquer, varnish, or shellac over it *after* it's fully dried.

You should also be aware that there is plastic cane on the market. It doesn't look as good, but it's stronger and easier to weave. It is handled the same way, except it doesn't need dampening.

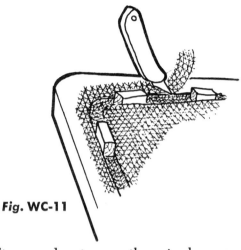

Fig. **WC-11**

For those who aren't very adventurous, there is also pre-woven cane that can be bought just like fabric. If the chair originally had this, it will have wooden splines that go in grooves to hold it in place. You'll probably have to buy new splines where you buy the prewoven cane. It will need to be soaked to make it pliable enough to bend around to fit in the groove. Make a pattern of the opening, plus the groove, plus two inches. Cut the prewoven cane to this pattern. Soak this in warm water to soften it, and then center it over the opening. Tape it in place. Select a blunt scrap of hardwood that will fit in the groove. Use this and a hammer to force the cane into the groove. Cut some blocks to spline size, and as you go along, tap these part way in to hold the cane in place in the groove. Remove the tape as you go along. When it's in the groove all the way around, take a very sharp utility knife as shown in Fig. WC-11 and cut off the overlap. Squeeze glue into the groove and start putting the spline in place. Tap it in, but not all the way. Remove the blocks as you go. When the spline is in all the way around, tap it down all the way. This pulls the cane tight, and then when the cane dries, it'll be tight as a drum.

If the previous cane wasn't prewoven, and you want to use this type as replacement, sew it in place much as we did with the binder. Then cover the holes with a binder.

Now that you can see how easy caning can be, why not get a kit and cane away! With just a little practice, you can be tops at bottoms.

Chapter 19

Outdoor Furniture

You already know that the big thing in outdoor furniture is weather. That includes rain, wind, sun, blowing sand, and whatever else Mother Nature decides to toss at it. Whether the furniture is metal, wood, or plastic, the finish is going to be attacked by both sun and rain. If it is wood, the wood itself can be rotted, swollen, warped, or discolored by moisture. Metal furniture is subject to rust. Canvas is subject to fading from the sun and rot and shrinkage from moisture. Stuffing can swell up or lump up from moisture, and if it does get wet, it's a whale of a job to ever get dry. Add all the weather problems to the fact that we tend to treat outdoor furniture with very little respect, and you've got an idea of why it can need help.

The key to coping with outdoor furniture problems lies in the selection of materials when you buy the furniture. But . . . you say you already have the furniture, and now you have to make it look good again? Okay. We'll try to give you a few pointers and also a few tips to keep from having to fix and finish quite so often.

WOOD

Of the woods found on patios, redwood is probably the most popular. When it's new, even though it's unfinished, it looks great. Redwood is resistant to rot. However, after a while it starts turning dark. Also, if it's not well made and held together with proper hardware, it can get wobbly. If that hardware isn't rust-resistant, it, too, will leave its mark. So a sealer of some sort is called for. However, once you put any kind of finish on, it's got to be refinished at least every year.

Redwood also doesn't swell when wet and doesn't warp easily. So why not leave it as is? Lots of people do . . . but just remember that the bare wood will absorb all the booze and food stains as well as dirt. (Avoid unfinished wood pieces near a pool . . . the chlorine splashes leave spots.) So if you're going to enjoy your wood furniture, I recommend a redwood sealer. A quick, light sanding is all the preparation needed. In applying, coat *everything* . . . the underneath sides too. And don't forget the bottoms of legs. They're on the ground or floor, and therefore have easiest access to moisture. As mentioned earlier, once done you'll have to do it annually . . . or maybe even once a year. Some people use a sealer with a redwood stain. This leaves an almost too-red look that takes a while for Mother Nature to tone down. Others use what's called a bleaching oil. It doesn't bleach all the color out, but rather gives it a weathered look . . . and at the same time has sealed the wood.

In addition, there are devotees of the use of spar varnish on any wood that's outside and is not to be painted. It does give the wood a tough weather- and people-resistant finish.

Any kind of wood can be used outside if it's sealed against the weather, and thus we find lots of painted patio pieces. In refinishing outdoor painted pieces, use the same ground rules as with any painting. If the piece has been subjected to moisture, make sure it's completely dried out. Any good enamel paint specified for outdoor use is okay. The glossier finishes keep looking better longer. A second coat makes sense here. Between paintings, keep on the lookout for cracks, gouges, or scuffed places that would allow moisture to get in. Check the tip ends of legs regularly and give them an extra coat of sealer if there's any chance these contact points can take on water.

No matter what kind of wood is involved, it will do better if the legs are up off the patio. This means glides or casters. The reason is that the legs dry faster when they don't drink up moisture from the patio surface. However, you want to make sure whatever hardware you do install in the legs won't rust and won't scratch up the patio.

Ping-Pong Tables — Several times, harried handymen have written to me asking what mix to use to get that "just right" shade of green to refinish a Ping-Pong table. Good news! You can buy it already mixed, and most paint manufacturers call it something like "Ping-Pong Table Green." If you make your own Ping-Pong table, be sure to use outside plywood . . . even if it's for an inside game room now. You may move and want it on the patio. Also, outdoor Ping-Pong tables can be helped in weathering the weather if you'll occasionally apply a light coat of boiled linseed oil. Be sure to wipe off the excess.

RATTAN AND WICKER FURNITURE

Rattan and wicker furniture are not my cup of tea. They're difficult to keep clean, and after a week or two all the tightening you've done seems to be of no avail . . . they wobble. Usually cleaning has to be a two-phase job . . . vacuuming the dust out and then washing with a damp rag and mild detergent. Never let this stuff stay soaking wet very long. This type furniture gives in to water more easily, and once inside, the moisture turns the wood an ugly black. Since most of this furniture is natural finish, the black isn't what you would call a decorator's touch. Chlorine bleach from the kitchen will remove the spots. A sealer followed by clear varnish is going to protect and leave the natural look. However, if you'll settle for paint, the black stains can just be left on and covered over. Just make sure the piece is completely dry. When this stuff starts to droop and sag in the seat, moisten with a vinegar and water solution and let dry in the sun. It may shrink. It may also require refinishing.

When an end comes loose, it should immediately be glued, tacked, or nailed back in place. If it's a binding strip, it may start to unravel. Twist it back tight and wrap thread around the end to hold it. Then dip it in clear shellac or glue. When it dries, reattach it.

Grapevine can be bent and formed to provide decorative braces for wicker furniture. It bends while still green, or if it has dried out, you can moisten with warm water to make the vines pliable again. Once shaped, it can be tacked in place.

But all-in-all, this type furniture is not too successful outside.

Chapter **20**

Metal Furniture

Not all furniture is made of wood. Some furniture is basically wood, but may have a glass or marble top. The fact that it's not wood doesn't mean you won't have problems.

Metal furniture is most often found on the patio. However, new designs in metal are not only acceptable but actually very "in"-looking in contemporary settings. Most metal furniture gives no trouble if it's protected from rust and corrosion. So mainly, metal furniture needs only care.

CHROME

If it's chrome, and a good chrome, it could last forever without ever being troubled by rust and corrosion. (However, don't buy chrome furniture if you live on the coast . . . the salt water is murder on it.) Otherwise, chrome care boils down to keeping it clean and taking care of scratches. You can get a chrome cleaning and polishing solution at an auto supply store. Follow the directions . . . or you can apply enough rubbing alcohol to dampen a rag, which does a good job. Another home chrome cleaner is Calgon and warm water. Wipe it dry.

If there's real dirt on the chrome, you may have to use detergent, but this has to be followed by the stuff from the auto store, rubbing alcohol, or Calgon because detergent leaves streaks. Scratched chrome is best treated with a spray-on chrome protector that is also available at the auto supply store. This protects the metal underneath from rust. However, if you're already too late and rust has started, it must be removed. Don't use steel wool, which will remove the rust and quite a bit of the chrome around the scratch. Scrape along the scratch with the point of a toothpick dipped in penetrating oil. Another way is to rub over the scratch with a crumpled piece of aluminum foil. When the rust is removed, clean, and then spray on the protector. In a pinch, clear nail polish over a scratch will prevent rust from getting started. After the chrome is clean, apply a coat of wax and polish it. This will keep it looking good and protect it too.

WROUGHT IRON

If it's iron, you've got to protect it yourself. Wrought iron has to be painted. To start with, a primer coat of rust preventive is needed. This is covered by the desired color which should also have rust-preventive qualities. For refinishing wrought iron if the old finish is sound, just spray or brush another coat over the old after scuff sanding.

One of my readers, who had wrought iron furniture with lots of legs, decided to cut out the high cost of spray-painting them. He also didn't like the overspray that kept getting on his car. Rather than try to brush all those legs, which would have taken hours, he bought a large powder puff. He poured the paint into a flat container, donned a rubber glove, and dipped the puff into the paint. He claims the paint went on smoothly and quickly . . . and his car is all one color.

If rust has started, you'll have to take a wire brush and remove all the rust. Then come in with the rust-preventive primer coat, followed by the finish coat. A coat of wax over the finish coat is a good idea. Between paintings, if you spot a chipped place, go over it with a crayon the same color as the finish. This will hide the chip and also keep rust out. Lazier handymen have been able to get away with this crayon treatment for several years before actually having to repaint. Of course, when it's repaint time, all the wax from the crayon has to be removed. Wrought iron breaks can be rewelded. Sometimes you can luck out and mend a break with epoxy metal cement. However, welding is usually better.

ALUMINUM

Of the metals, aluminum is the most trouble-free. (It won't rust, but can pit and corrode.) Aluminum is popular as patio and deck furniture because it's rustproof and lightweight. In fact, it's lightweight enough that it can get knocked or blown over and bent. (Don't leave lightweight aluminum pieces near the pool. They always blow in.) But extra weight can be added to some tubular pieces by pouring sand into the lower parts. Naturally, don't do this unless the sand can be capped in.

Keep tips on those tubular legs to prevent scratch-up of the patio . . . and fraying of your nerves. (If they're rubber tips, place washers in them to keep the tubes from cutting through.) Plastic caps from many medicine bottles can be glued in place as tips.

Some patio furniture is made of bent aluminum tubing, and the legs are runners that rest on the floor. Every time you move one of these pieces, the noise makes your teeth hurt. Slit lengths of garden hose can fit over the runners and will remove the noise as well as the possibility of scratching up your patio.

Natural aluminum can oxidize, which starts pitting and turns the shine off with a whitish residue. Once this starts, you probably need to remove it with steel wool. However, before you get into that, crumple a piece of aluminum foil and rub at the spots with this. Once it's clean, put on a protective coating of either wax or spray lacquer. The latter is naturally going to last a lot longer.

FOLDING FURNITURE

And here's a word about folding lawn furniture—"Ouch!" Even when all the moving parts are working freely, you may not be able to fold or unfold a chair. They never seem to be made to push the way they look like they should be pushed. This can make you look like a real dummy. When the joints are not properly lubricated, you may never even know which is the right way. Where possible, use a wax or a silicone spray. Then if you ever do get the things set up, you won't get oily spots on your clothes. If you do get "bitten" while trying to handle one of these monsters, it's customary to keep it under observation for fourteen days to see if it's rabid.

One guy fights the unfolding problem by adding little colored plastic handles. He knows to always pull the blue tab first, then the red, then green, etc.

Here are just a few random rules of thumb and helpful hints on care of your outdoor furniture:

1. Keep them out of the elements as much as possible.
2. Clean furniture regularly so that dirt, droppings, and food can't start attacking the finish.
3. Use only waterproof adhesives in repairs.
4. Dry all furniture as soon as possible after a rain.
5. Always use rustproof hardware in repair and building.
6. Drill a few holes in curved metal seats so water can't stand in them.
7. Don't invite Dick Butkus to your garden party . . .

Chapter 21

Outdoor Upholstery

First of all, any furniture with cloth involved should be protected from rain. If you have a trick knee that lets you know ahead of time that it's going to rain, cover the pieces or bring the cushions in.

Make or buy plastic covers for the pieces that can't be moved in. Cheap plastic drop cloths can be taped or weighted in place. If the fabrics do get wet, dry them out as soon as possible.

Canvas that fades can be painted with a special canvas paint.

And boiled linseed oil brushed on canvas lawn furniture will give it longer life and waterproof the fabric. (Be sure to let dry before sitting on it, or your chair will want to follow you inside.)

A good waterproofing concoction for outdoor fabrics in general is made by dissolving paraffin in turpentine. Use a potato peeler and shave thin slivers of the wax (one-quarter pound total) into a quart of turpentine. To help dissolve the wax, place this container in a large pan of very hot water. (Never use an open flame.) When the paraffin is melted, brush this generously on canvas lawn furniture, and you'll triple the life of the fabric.

Director's chairs and campaign chairs are popular patio pieces. The canvas replacement sets are available at most outdoor furniture shops. If they don't have the color you want, however, you can buy the fabric and make your own, using the old covers as a pattern. You probably won't save any money, but if you can't find a ready-made to match your eyes, it's worth it.

Torn places can be mended by sewing or by using press-on patches. Since the press-ons are popular now, there are lots of designs, and the mending can also be a decorating process. If any fabrics are shot and have to be replaced, try to use the old pieces as your pattern. Also, try to replace the fabric with some sort of vinyl or other plastic.

PLASTIC FABRICS

Vinyl is a widely used plastic fabric because it's rugged, stain resistant, and looks a little like leather. It can become dirty, but that's no problem. Usually, synthetic fabrics can be kept clean with just a damp cloth. If there seem to be stubborn dirt spots, wash the surface with a mild detergent. Then hose 'em off.

If they become ripped, there is plastic mending adhesive on the market. It's possible to mend a torn spot by gluing the edges together, but this repair usually won't last. Patches do best. If you can get vinyl to match, follow the instructions on the tube of adhesive and patch holes or rips. It's less obtrusive if you can do it from underneath. Since most vinyl-covered furniture is in a casual setting, if the patches show up too much, hide them with plastic stick-ons. They come in several wild designs and are pressure sensitive . . . or make your own stick-ons from vinyl scraps and apply with the adhesive.

Webbing — Furniture with plastic webbing is usually fairly trouble-free until all of a sudden two of the webbing strips give way. You probably won't be able to patch it up, but try if you wish. Once you're convinced, go buy a rewebbing kit. They're very inexpensive, and it's fairly easy to reweb this furniture. The kits have good instructions.

Rewebbing folding lawn furniture is actually easier than unfolding the chair. With a metal frame, the webbing is attached in several different ways. Washerhead screws such as shown in Fig. RW-1 are often used. There are also some little gizmos called reweb clips as shown in Fig. RW-2 that do the job

Fig. RW-2

Fig. RW-1

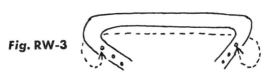

Fig. RW-3

by replacing screws. Of course the webbing can be sewed together using nylon or Dacron thread.

On wooden-framed chairs, all of these methods except clips can be used, or the webbing can be fastened with tacks.

If screws or clips were used originally, stick with them. However, if sewing or tacking was used, you might want to think about switching to clips or screws.

The first step is to determine how much new webbing is needed. For the screw type, measure from the screw hole on one side around the frame and over to the screw hole on the opposite frame (Fig. RW-3). Add three and a half inches. This gives you the length of each cross strip. Multiply times the number of cross strips. Now, determine the length of the strips going the other way. Add the three and a half inches and multiply this times the number of strips. Add the two figures together, and you'll know how much webbing you'll need. (This same formula works if you're going to use tacks.)

For clips, measure from the slot or hole under the tube to the opposite slot. However, add only one and a half inches to each strip.

If you're going to sew, just determine how much material it will take to loop around the frame on each side, and give yourself some room to sew through.

For the screws and tacks, the webbing needs to be folded over as shown in Fig. RW-4, and the screw or tack placed

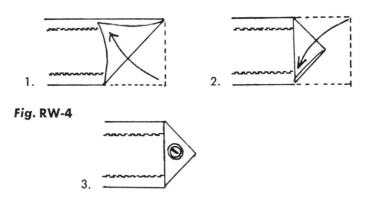

Fig. RW-4

through the fold. If you don't have washerhead screws, a washer should be used.

Sometimes the screw holes get too large to hold. You can either go to larger screws or opt for clips. The points of the clips fit into the screwholes or into slots if the piece had been webbed with clips originally. Fig. RW-5 shows how the clips fit in and how the webbing is folded.

Fig. RW-5

Chapter 22

Nonwood Tabletops

MARBLE TOPS ─────────────────

Not much matches the luxury look attained by a marble tabletop. Even though it looks as if nothing could penetrate its surface, marble stains fairly easily. Marble can better resist stains if it's kept properly sealed. Marble sealer is available at stores that sell marble pieces. I think most of them recommend resealing about twice a year, but wipe up any spills as quickly as possible.

Some things that don't stain will etch the surface and leave dull spots. Try a plain damp cloth first. If that doesn't cut it, use a detergent that is mild. There are special marble detergents also available, and if you're really sloppy and have to clean up daily, I'd get this stuff. It won't yellow the marble the way too much household detergent can.

Never wash marble while there is grit on it as it scratches easily. Blow off or vacuum away the grit.

Most tougher stains can be removed from marble with hydrogen peroxide and ammonia. However, the kind of peroxide you buy from the drug store usually isn't strong enough, although it's worth a try before you go to the tombstone maker. The special marble peroxide is about 35 percent. The way to do it is to use a rag folded over several times. Soak it in the peroxide and place it over the spot. Now put several drops of household ammonia on this pad. When it stops bubbling, wipe it off with a damp cloth. If the stain is still there, you might try again or try to get a stronger hydrogen peroxide. There are also several different brands of commercial-type marble cleaning solutions on the market. If you're going to have to go to a marble dealer anyway, this may be your best bet.

Scratches are also a common marble malady. Even though it may scratch easily, it doesn't buff that easily. It's hard work and takes time. Tiny scratches can be buffed out with a powder called tin oxide and a damp buffing pad. The pad can be felt, chamois, or even a scrap of hard wool carpeting. Keep adding a few drops of water to keep the powder lubricated. Larger scratches may require use of a fine sandpaper before getting to the tin oxide powder. If so, I'd suggest you get a marble polishing kit. It will have special abrasive stones to be used in sequence from coarse to fine. It will also have instructions on how to use everything in the kit. Really bad scratches are better done by a pro . . . who cheats and uses a machine that takes a little off the entire top.

Broken marble slabs can be glued back together. Clean and dry the edges and use epoxy cement. The two pieces should be firmly clamped together. Masking tape will usually do the job. Now give it a full twenty-four hours to set up.

PLASTIC LAMINATES

Nowadays, lots of high-use pieces of furniture have tops covered with plastic laminates such as Formica. Bar tops, desk tops and tabletops are rendered stainproof and almost scratch-proof when this strong, durable material is used. You already know from the kitchen that this stuff is easy to clean. A damp sponge with mild detergent or even a kitchen cleansing powder can be used. However, if you do put a hole or dent in a laminate top, you've had it.

Stick shellac that matches the color is my choice for repair. (See Part Two.) Some people will cut out the bad spot and put in a patch. At best, it sticks out like a sore thumb. If you want to try it in spite of this, first make sure you can get a patch to match. A rectangular pattern will be the easiest shape to dupli-cate, so mark one around the bad place. Before it's attached to the piece of furniture, plastic laminate is easy to cut. Now that it's down, it's next to impossible. The easiest way is to cut all the way through and remove the structure underneath. With this out, the bad piece can be pried off, and the new patch applied to the block. Remember to make the patch as big as the opening, which will be a little larger than the block of wood. Also, you'll have to plug the hole in the block that you made so you could get the saw blade in. Use laminate cement, following the instructions as to pressure and waiting time. Now work the piece in place and glue the wood block back in place. Any cracks in the top can be filled with stick shellac. Some folks just cut out the piece of laminate with a chisel. Use a sharp one and let the bevel face in toward the damaged area.

Once the piece is cut all the way around, run a torch across it quickly a few times to soften the adhesive. Then pry it out and glue the new one back in place following the recommended procedures. Remember to be sure to remove the old mastic. Be careful not to burn the good part of the top with the torch, and don't expect to have a totally invisible patch . . . did I talk you out of it? (Maybe you can figure out how to keep a lamp or ash tray over the damaged spot and not have to repair it. . . .)

The only other thing that happens to laminates is that they can come loose from the wooden base. No big deal. Scrape out as much of the old adhesive as possible and then vacuum out the scrapings. Use laminate cement, but not the contact kind. Follow the instructions as to application, waiting time, and pressure.

PLASTIC FURNITURE

Some great-looking outdoor tables come with glass tops. To my way of thinking, it makes more sense to opt for acrylic plastic sheet material instead of glass . . . particularly around a pool. Slivers of broken glass hide for years until your foot finally picks them up . . . one by one. Now you're probably wondering just what acrylic plastic sheet is . . . if I'd said Plexiglas you'd have known right off. There are other brands besides Plexiglas, but since everyone knows what we're talking about, I'll refer to that brand by its registered name. And the dealer will sell you whatever acrylic sheet goods he has.

Plexiglas is almost unbreakable, but if you invited Dick

Butkus to your pool party, and he smashed your tabletop, it would break into fairly large pieces. It's virtually weather-resistant and doesn't stain easily. However, it can become scratched . . . but then so can most furniture. Only with Plexiglas, the scratches come out.

Little ones disappear with a little auto paste wax applied with a soft clean cloth. Then buff with a clean cotton flannel rag. Readers of my column have suggested the use of both tooth powder and toothpaste to remove scratches. Rub with a damp rag. This works and also fights cavities if you use the fluoride kind. Deeper scratches need a light sanding with a superfine sandpaper and then buffing with a fine grit buffing compound. After the scratches are gone, apply an overall coat of auto paste wax to protect the surface. Next wipe the surface with a clean damp cloth to do away with static electricity. Paint or heavy grease spots come off with kerosene. Never use kitchen scouring powders or strong solvents such as gasoline, carbon tet, alcohol, or acetone.

Chapter 23

Instant Furniture

Although you probably won't win any design awards, there are a number of furniture pieces that can be thrown together in moments and with little effort or investment.

I guess the earliest instant bookshelf idea we ever used was the bricks and boards shelves shown in Fig. IF-1. We spent a little dough for oak boards, but most homes will have planks around. One-by-twelves are best in most cases, but you may find looks or space dictate a narrower shelf. This is really a good help for apartment dwellers where the landlord frowns on any kind of attached shelves, and where you can't afford an outlay of heavy cash.

Those big wooden electric cable spools are instant patio furniture. Industrial electrical contractors, Ma Bell, and utility companies have them. They are not easy to come by. However, they are great because the really big size is a table, and the smaller size is perfect for chairs. The chairs need a cushion, but the table can get by as is. If you wish, you could cut a round top of masonite for the table. Painted to your taste, you've got a sturdy set of outdoor furniture.

Great looking sturdy stools can be made from sections of that

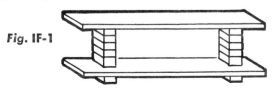

Fig. **IF-1**

159

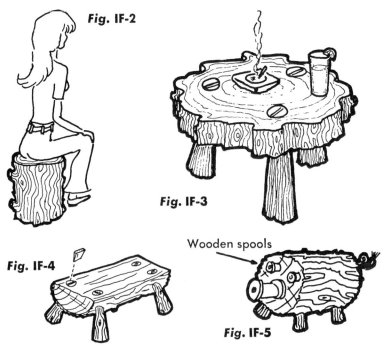

Fig. IF-2

Fig. IF-3

Fig. IF-4

Wooden spools

Fig. IF-5

big old oak tree that died (Fig. IF-2). Just cut 'em off to the proper height. As long as you've chopped the tree up, here are self-explanatory sketches of a table (Fig. IF-3), a stool with legs (Fig. IF-4), and a kooky pig made from logs (Fig. IF-5). Another nice thing about this furniture is that when you tire of it, it goes into the fireplace on a chilly evening. (I've wanted to end several of my projects this way!)

A not-quite-so-instant patio bench is shown in Fig. IF-6. The larger solar screen blocks are of concrete and come in several designs. A masonry drill bit makes holes in the blocks so the seat may be bolted on. The seat is formed by a pair of two-by-eights of redwood. A longer bench might need additional concrete blocks in the center for more stability.

Many breakables are still shipped in small wooden barrels. If you can get your hands on some of these, they can be almost instantly converted to rustic patio or den stools as shown in Fig. IF-7.

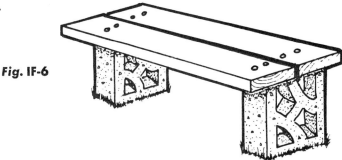

Fig. IF-6

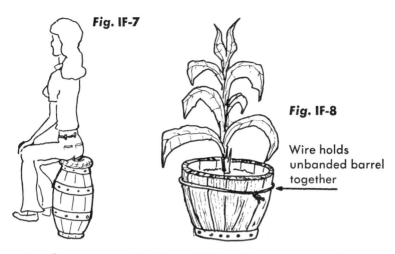

Fig. IF-7

Fig. IF-8

Wire holds
unbanded barrel
together

Another great use for these old barrels is to convert them to patio planter boxes. Cut the barrel in half after putting on a wire binding as shown in Fig. IF-8. To prepare the surface inside so it won't get fungus from the moist dirt, do as one reader suggested. Squirt charcoal lighter fluid all around on the inside. Step back and toss a match into the barrel halves. When the fire has charred the wood inside, douse the flame by putting a sheet of metal or old plywood right on top, shutting off the oxygen. Naturally, you want to do this outside and keep well back when you first ignite the fire . . . and don't wait so long that you burn your planter to the ground.

Leftover chair and table legs can be converted to very decorative lamps. For the lamp shown in Fig. IF-9, all that was

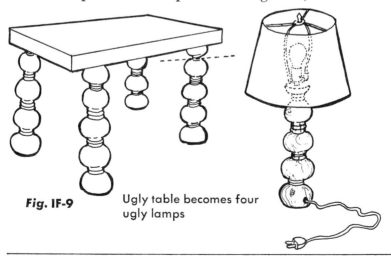

Fig. IF-9   Ugly table becomes four ugly lamps

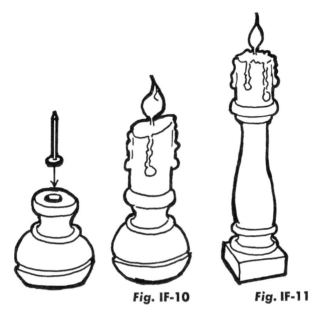

Fig. IF-10   **Fig. IF-11**

done was to cut off the leg to the desired height, and drill a hole through the leg for the cord. Another hole, as shown, was drilled to allow the cord to come out at the side. Some legs would not be large enough at the bottom to stand alone without a base. A square block of wood attached to the bottom will solve this problem. The lamp hardware and cord are available at your friendly hardware dealer. A shade can be found at most stores that carry lamps.

The old finish of the chair or table may be just what you're looking for in a lamp, or you may want to refinish.

To make legs into candle holders, about all you need to do is finish the cut-off leg and install a nail in the top to hold the candle. You just drill a hole in the top and insert the nail with the point out. Wood putty or filler will hold the nail in place. When it's set up, you're ready to impale the candle and drag out the wine (Fig. IF-10 and IF-11).

WHAT YOU CAN DO WITH YOUR PIANO ⸻

Lots of folks have an old monster piano down in the basement getting uglier. It's teeth are turning yellow, its skin is beginning to look like alligator's hide, and it is probably totally inaccessible in case Van Cliburn happens to drop in.

I haven't the foggiest notion of how to tune it or make it playable, but there are lots of exciting things to do on the outside to make it worthy of a place in the den.

We had a perfectly plain spinet that had once been sterile white. The lines were of the sort popular in furniture of the late thirties, sometimes called "Depression Modern." It didn't fit with all our Mexican furniture. By the simple addition of some Mexican-looking plant-ons, a little molding, and an antiquing kit, we made it look like it came from Guadalajara. We found some old brass drawer pulls in the Thieves' Market in Mexico City, and Jean recovered the seat in a scrap of nubby fabric to complete the transformation.

We do keep it closed to hide the yellow teeth. However, keys, both black and white—or yellow, can be recovered. There are also polishing kits for ivory which will do the job if the stain is just on the surface.

Even if you don't want the Latin look, the addition of plant-ons, molding, and hardware can start the project. Other face-lifts could involve a new veneer, contact paper, mirror squares, Formica, or even carpeting. If you just wish to refinish, treat the wood as any other piece of furniture.

The only precautions are to make sure any surface covering you add won't interfere with the movement of the keys and pedals.

If you're sure Van Cliburn won't drop in, and you have no desire to ever play again, do as one friend did. He converted an old upright into a bar with shelves for glasses and bottles inside. That still left room for an ice chest. He actually enjoys his piano more than most people do.

A bass drum that has lost its boom can become a real conversation piece of a coffee table. Cut a plywood circle to fit over the head, refinish the rest, and you're ready to serve coffee (Fig. IF-12). If the drum head hasn't been busted, a Plexiglas circle will do. Where do you get a drum? Junior high schools run through them pretty fast, and music stores sometimes take trade-ins that can't be "reboomed."

Fig. IF-12

PLEXIGLAS

Incidentally, making furniture from Plexiglas is a fun project and easy to do. Such furniture isn't exactly instant, but some pieces are easy to whip up. The places that sell the sheet stock also have an excellent little book that tells how to work in this medium. They also have the few tools that help your project turn out like the pictures in the book.

For example, the end table shown in Fig. IF-13 can be made in about an hour (exclusive of finishing). The wooden dividers are turnings that can be bought at lumberyards and home centers. The feet and finials are threaded and go together as shown. The two shelves are cut from ¼-inch sheet stock. Appropriate-sized holes are drilled for the threaded parts. The edges are smoothed and buffed, and the piece is put together.

Other projects call for bending Plexiglas, and some for gluing pieces together. Because of its transparency, Plexiglas can be formed into all sorts of elegant pedestals, coffee tables, and end pieces which you can fill partly with earth and plant with tropical whatnots. Just be sure your bottom seals are watertight—a layer of fiber glass or epoxy around the bottom is a good idea, and since the dirt inside is black anyway, it won't show. If placed near a window, your plants inside should really take off, but do be sure the top slab is removable for weeding and pruning. Because of the sealed greenhouse effect, you'll need water only once in quite a while.

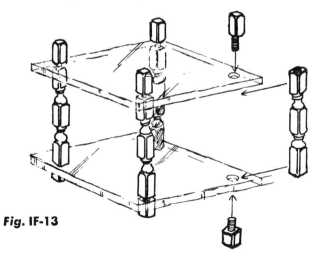

Fig. IF-13

One merry character in Arizona has a Plexiglas coffee table lined with sand and featuring a live sidewinder. It's quite a sight at cocktail parties, he says, to have that little critter buzzing away underneath a martini. (When the party gets dull, he just slips in a white mouse . . .) So here are some basics on cutting, drilling, finishing, cementing, and forming this material.

Plexiglas can be cut with a saber saw or band saw, which means you can cut it to any desired shape. The first rule is to leave the protective paper backing in place on the plastic until all the sawing, drilling, and smoothing is done. Use a blade with fourteen or more teeth per inch with saber saws, and at least ten teeth per inch with a band saw. Be sure the sheet is placed on a smooth surface, and hold it down firmly while cutting. Don't force feed—easy does it.

Drilling can be done with either hand or power drills. With a twist drill, use a sharp bit, back the work with a soft wood block, and clamp it in place. Go slow, and don't push down with any more force than you need just to keep the drill in position. For a power drill, buy a special bit specified for acrylic plastic sheet. Back with a soft wood block, and clamp. High speed is best here if you have a variable speed drill. However, don't force feed.

Edges can be smoothed by sanding. Use a medium grit first, and then finish with superfine. Some people use buffing compound as the last step to end up with a transparent edge.

As for bending, heat is the answer. However, the home handyperson should limit his bending projects to straight-line bends and use thinner plastic sheets—say ¼-inch or less. The best way to go is to buy a strip heater element made for just this purpose. It's an inexpensive little narrow web belt with an electric plug on the end. You do need to construct a heater unit so that the plastic doesn't actually touch the element. It's a simple job involving plywood scraps, aluminum foil, asbestos paper, and maybe fifteen minutes of time. The instructions come with the element. I do suggest that you practice bending on scraps of plastic first. This will let you know the heating element is far enough away not to bubble the plastic. Also, a little practice will let you know exactly when to make the bend

. . . if it's made too early, you get a crazed effect inside the plastic all along the bend.

You face the outside of the bend toward the element, and when it is thoroughly heated along the line, you'll see it soften. Slow, gentle bending is all it takes. Then move it away from the element, get it at just the right angle, and hold it there until it cools.

As for gluing, I have used a number of adhesives with varying results. In most cases, you want a bond that itself is as nearly transparent as possible. There are several clear cements on the market that specify that they are for use on plastics. They work. However, the best go is a special cement called WELD-ON 3, made for this purpose alone. It's a thin liquid that dries fast and is completely transparent. If it's a project where transparency doesn't count, contact cements and mastics like you use for ceiling tiles, plywood panels, or floor tiles will hold tight—even if Dick Butkus does show up.

Chapter 24

Final Advice

Now that you've gone this far, you should have gained a lot of confidence and a little knowledge. If you don't want to make furniture, there are a million or so already made pieces just waiting to be refinished. This may require only a coat of paint, or may allow you to completely redesign the piece to look like you. (Personally, I'd hate to have a hall tree that looked like me.) But if you have done nothing more than fix up the old Early Poverty furniture you have had around all along, you know that three or four years from now when you desire a change, you can do it. We have some old pieces that we have stripped so often they start to shiver at the whiff of lye. Each new color scheme seems to call for a change of furniture, and it's a lot cheaper to change the finish than change the furniture.

If the idea of fixing and finishing furniture grabs you, there are all sorts of ways to push ahead. You can get involved in making your own furniture without being a designer, either. You can get plans for just about any piece in any style. Or you could copy a piece you like. Whatever course you do take . . . be sure you work from plans.

POWER TOOLS

If you're going to advance into making furniture, you can make many chores go faster and easier with power. This requires an investment, but the enjoyment is fantastic. You can drown out all woes with the buzz of a saw or chatter of a router.

Other power tools can help. A grinding wheel helps keep tools sharp. A portable electric jigsaw or saber saw can do some plain and fancy cutting, but you don't have to have it. A router is great to have for joints, as well as decorative cuts, but again, you don't have to have it. A lathe is one power tool whose work can't be duplicated by hand, but unless you're going to turn lots of spindles, it's not practical to own one.

I've already mentioned that an electric drill is almost a basic. If you're buying a new one, spend a little extra and get a variable speed job.

However, you don't have to have electricity in the house to do furniture fixing. Many fine craftsmen will use power for rough work, but wouldn't think of using anything but hand tools for finished work.

So power is strictly an option—nice to have, but for most furniture fixin', it ain't necessarily necessary.

But you might appreciate a few tips on tools we haven't mentioned up to now. You won't need them all, though, and you can decide as you go along just how involved you wish to be. (Again, if all you're going to do is paint and decorate mass-produced unfinished furniture, then you'll need practically no tools and very few materials.)

Whocking Tools —

Hammers   Except for driving nails underneath on frames where no one will see, a regular carpenter's hammer does more harm than good.

Tack hammers   The magnetic tip makes it a must for reupholstering. The magnet holds the tack until it's hammered in. (Sure saves the smashed fingers.)

Mallets   These come with faces of rawhide, rubber, wood, and plastic so you can tap without marring, or, you can make a mallet out of your regular hammer by slipping a rubber crutch tip over the head.

Measuring — A retractable metal tape, a steel rule, and a metal square will be handy. *Never* use a cloth tape measure from the sewing basket. It can stretch and make grossly inaccurate measurements. This is particularly bad news when you're trying to replace a part.

WHAT ELSE?

Hardware stores are full of tools that would be helpful. If you get hooked on fixing and making furniture, you'll eventually run across such mail-order tool suppliers as Brookstone and Constantine. They, and other specialty tool houses, have so many unusual gadgets and hardware you'll drool on the pages of their catalogs.

But whatever you do, invest in good tools. Quality tools will last longer and help you do a better job. As a general rule, stick with well-known brand names. Or if it's a private label, make sure the store will stand behind it. A good hardware dealer will give you an honest rundown on the various brands he carries.

Also, after you've bought these quality tools, take care of them. Make sure they are properly stored to protect them. Keep them lubricated, and remember: all cutting tools are safer and more efficient when properly sharpened.

In some cases, you'll want to take all the know-how and experience you got here and get into restoration of antiques. There are many good books that deal specifically with restoration. It can be a profitable hobby as well as providing you with a well-furnished home.

But the collecting of antique furniture requires a tremendous knowledge, or you can be had rather badly. Still, the knowledge of repair and refinishing can also help the new collector to spot fakes or pieces that have been over-repaired, thus reducing the value. And knowing about repairs and refinishing can also help you to determine *whether* the piece can be restored. So after you have decided it's an authentic Queen Ann whatyoumaycallit, it still may be of little value if it can't be whipped into shape. (You see why I avoid priceless antiques . . . whipping them never seems to enhance their value.)

Whatever you do in future furniture efforts, I hope you will look back on our time together with fondness. Good luck!

SEMI-GLOSSARY
(Not a dull finish, we hope)

ABRASIVES Any of the smoothing products: sandpaper, steel wool, pumice, and all that jazz.

ADHESION The stick-ability of one coat over another or to the material underneath.

AIR DRY The ability of a coating to reach its proper hardness in normal atmospheric conditions.

ANILINE DYE Aniline is a coal tar derivative and creates a soluble when used in an oil base.

APPLIQUE See *Plant-ons*.

APRON A strip of wood around the edge of a table or other flat furniture.

BANANA OIL Amyl acetate, a colorless solvent and vehicle for lacquer.

BASE COAT This is the first coat of the actual finish color.

BENZINE Naphtha made from coal tar.

BENZOL Naphtha made from coal tar.

BITE The act of softening the preceding coat by the next coat.

BLEEDING What happens when something underneath shows through the layers on top.

BOILED LINSEED OIL No! Don't you go boil it. This refers to a process at the factory, and you ask for it that way at the paint or hardware store. It has faster "dryability" than regular linseed oil.

BRIDGING The act of filling over minor indentations by a coating.

BURNISHING Rubbing with a hard smooth tool for an added sheen.

CARNAUBA WAX A yellow, very hard wax, also called Brazilian wax.

CATALYTICS A two-part finish—a separate hardener is mixed in.

CHAMFER A beveled cut.

CHINAWOOD OIL Tung oil.

CRAZING Fine-lined cracks in a very old finish.

CUT See *Shellac*.

DADO A rectangular groove cut across the grain the full width of the board.

DOWEL A round length of wood.

DOWEL JOINT A joint where a round peg of one part fits and is glued into a hole in the adjoining part.

DRIERS Compounds that can be added to some finishes to speed drying time. Most store-bought finishes already have maximum driers added. Read the label to see which driers to use.

ENAMEL A name attached to colored gloss finishes.

EPOXY GLUE Two-part extra-hold adhesive.

EPOXY PAINT Same principle as the epoxy glue—very tough finish.

FEATHERING Blending of edges on a surface by abrasives to make unlike parts seem to flow together.

FILLERS Any of the pastelike substances used to fill pores in open-grained woods.

FLAT FINISH Nonglossy.

FLOAT As used with pumice, it is a grade—indicated as F, FF, or FFF to show single, double, or triple fineness.

GIMP A braidlike trim used in upholstery.

GLOSSY FINISH Shiny and reflective.

GRAIN The pattern in woods.

GRAINING Faking it to simulate a grain.

GUSSET A glue block.

HARDWOOD Name generally given to wood from broadleaf trees. Some hardwood isn't as hard as some softwood.

KD Knocked down—When you buy furniture, and it's to be shipped "KD," that means you'll do the assembling.

Kd Kiln-dried—as applies to lumber.

KERF The cut made by a saw.

LACQUER A solvent-evaporating coating that can be clear or colored.

LATEX A water-based paint that makes clean-up a cinch.

LINSEED OIL Made from flaxseed, it's the oldest natural wood preservative. Wonder why they don't call it flaxseed oil. (See *Boiled Linseed Oil*).

MATTE FINISH A nonglossy finish.

MINERAL SPIRITS An oil-derivative thinner.

NGR Non-grain-raising.

NAPHTHA A solvent and cleaner.

NIBS Boo-boos that happen when a finish rises to cover particles on the surface.

OPEN GRAIN Wood with open pores.

ORANGE SHELLAC The amber-colored shellac that is unbleached.

OVERCOATING Completely covering a surface to obscure the grain or old color.

PATINA   A word used by antique buffs to describe a quality of mellowness to an old, well-cared-for wood surface.

PENETRATING FINISHES   Those that sink into the wood, leaving little or no surface elements.

PLANT-ONS   Decorative sculptured pieces of wood or plastic that can be glued or nailed to furniture.

PORES   Tiny natural holes in wood.

PUMICE   A fine abrasive powder made from lava.

RABBET   A cut made on the edge of one board, sized to receive the end or edge of another.

RABBET JOINT   No, it's not a Playboy Club, but the joining of two pieces of wood, as above.

REDUCER   Another name for thinner.

RESIN   A natural or synthetic material used as a film-forming ingredient in paint.

RETARDER   Anything added to slow down the drying time.

ROSIN   A resin from wood.

ROTTENSTONE   Very fine powdered abrasive.

RUBBING OIL   Mineral oils used as lubricants when rubbing down a finish with fine abrasives.

RUNS   A boo-boo caused when the coat of paint or finish is put on too heavily to stay in place.

SAGS   See *Runs*.

SATIN FINISH   A silky sheen—shiny, but not reflective.

SEALER   Any coating that stops subsequent coats from penetrating the surface below or previous coats from bleeding through the coats above.

SETTING   The initial surface hardening of a film.

SHELLAC   A natural gum solution used as a finish.

SOFTWOOD   Name generally given to wood from trees that bear cones.

SOLVENT   A liquid that dissolves another substance.

SPAR VARNISH   Varnish for rugged or outdoor use.

STAIN   Anything that changes the natural color of the wood.

TSP   Trisodium phosphate.

TACK RAG   A lint-free, varnish-impregnated cloth used to remove dust.

TACKY   When a finish or adhesive is still sticky to the touch but doesn't stick to the finger.

THINNER   A compatible liquid used to thin another liquid.

TIPPING OFF   Smoothing a wet surface with just the tip of the brush barely touching the surface.

TURP   Short for turpentine.

VARNISH A resinous-based finishing material.

VENEER A thin layer of wood over a surface. Usually added to give beauty.

WELT A fabric-covered cord used to cover upholstery seams.

WET EDGE Application whereby one brush stroke is applied next to the previous one before it starts to dry.

WHITE SHELLAC The bleached kind.

WIPING STAINS Those brushed on and then wiped off.

Index

Abrasives, 54, 64, 68–71, 73, 88
Acetone, 56, 65, 158
Acrylic paint, 110
Acrylic plastic sheet, *see* Plexiglas
Adhesive, *see* Glue
Aging, artificial, 72
Alcohol, 59, 88–89, 123, 158
Alcohol burner, 52
Aluminum foil, 148–49, 165
Aluminum furniture, 149
Aluminum oxide cloth, 69
Aluminum oxide paper, 69, 88
Ammonia, 54, 62, 66–67, 78, 109,
    123–24, 155–56
Antique furniture, 62, 71–73, 169
Antiquing, 104–7, 112
Aprons, 21–22
Asbestos paper, 165
Ash wood, 34–35, 78, 81

Back saws, 38
Baking soda, cleaning with, 123
Ball peen hammer, 72
Band clamps, 9
Band saw, 165
Bar clamps, 8, 42
Barrels, 160–61
Baseball bats, 34

Basswood, 34–35, 75, 78
Beds, 116
Beech wood, 34–35, 78
Belt clamps, 9
Belt sander, 68–69
Bench planes, 41
Benzine, 65, 82
Birch wood, 34–35, 78
Bleach, 62, 66–67
Bleaching, 66
Bleaching oil, 144
Blisters, 2, 44
Block planes, 41
Bolts, 29, 57
Bookshelves, 159
Brace and bit, 14
Brads, 28
Bronzing, 108, 112
Brushes
    finishing and, 79–80, 88, 93,
      95–96
    gilding and, 109–11
    paint and, 99, 101–6
Bubbles, 44–45
Buffing, 55, 84, 156, 158
Bureaus, 21, 25
Burlap, 128, 132
Burnishing, 111